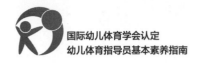

国际幼儿体育学会认定
幼儿体育指导员基本素养指南

幼儿体育与健康
—— 让孩子运动、心动、感动 ——

日本幼儿体育学会　前桥　明　著
（早稻田大学　教授·医学博士）

北京绿树体育　译

大学教育出版

幼儿体育与健康 — 让孩子运动、心动、感动

目　次

Part I （中　文）

生活作息对幼儿健康的重要性

－"吃好、睡好、运动好"的运动策略 － ·················· *3*

1. 近年来幼儿所面临的三个问题 ·················· *3*
   - （1） 睡眠节奏不规律··················*3*
   - （2） 饮食节奏的混乱··················*5*
   - （3） 运动不足 ··················*6*
2. 休息、营养、运动问题的出现与自主神经系统 ·················· *7*
3. 体温的变化规律 ·················· *8*
   - （1） 随着年龄增长体温的变化规律也不同 ··················*8*
   - （2） 低体温对身体的影响··················*8*
   - （3） 改善体温变化的方法··················*9*
   - （4） 体内生物钟与脑内荷尔蒙 ·················· *10*
   - （5） 午睡的作用 ·················· *10*
4. 睡眠进一步混乱带来的问题 ·················· *11*
5. 创造健康生活的建议 ·················· *11*
6. 近年来孩子们所存在的问题 ·················· *12*
7. 培养孩子健康全面发展的目标 ·················· *15*
8. 孩子的成长、发展状况的诊断和评价 ·················· *15*
   - （1） 睡眠・休养 ·················· *15*
   - （2） 营养・膳食 ·················· *16*
   - （3） 活动 ·················· *16*

（4）运动之基本 ················· *16*
　　（5）发展的均衡性
　　　　（身体的・社会的・智力的・精神的・情绪的发展）··· *17*
　　（6）父母的作用和帮助 ················· *18*
9. 现如今，如果您都厌倦了，那么孩子会变得很糟糕 ····· *18*

幼儿体育的意义与作用 ················· *20*
1. 幼儿体育的定义 ················· *20*
2. 幼儿体育的目标 ················· *21*
3. 幼儿体育的指导方法 ················· *21*
　　（1）指导方法 ················· *22*
　　（2）指导技巧 ················· *22*
4. 需要让孩子们体验的运动 ················· *23*
5. 对幼儿体育的期待 ················· *24*
6. 幼儿体育应有的状态 ················· *25*
7. 进行幼儿体育指导的注意事项 ················· *26*

幼儿体育需要了解的重点内容 ················· *28*
1. 幼儿体育的理论方面 ················· *28*
2. 幼儿体育的实践方面 ················· *35*

关于幼儿体育指导方法的见解 ················· *38*
1. 活动前的注意事项 ················· *38*
　　（1）创设安全的环境 ················· *38*

（2）	服装	39
（3）	指导者的站位	39
（4）	队形	40
（5）	整队与间距	40
（6）	准备活动	41
（7）	分组	41

2. 活动展开时的注意事项 ········· 42

（1）	说话方式	42
（2）	满足感	42
（3）	士气的鼓舞	42
（4）	培养主体性，自发性和创造力	43
（5）	应对危险	43
（6）	竞争	44
（7）	对有胆怯心理孩子的关注	44
（8）	运动量	44
（9）	辅助	45
（10）	技术的习得	45
（11）	注意力的持续	46
（12）	创造轻松愉快的气氛	46

3. 整理部分 ········· 46

（1）	整理运动	46
（2）	整理物品	47
（3）	活动的总结	47
（4）	运动后的安全和卫生保健	47

公园运动器材与孩子运动能力的培养 ·············· *49*

1. 夜晚型生活给孩子造成的消极影响 ··············· *49*
2. 过多地接触媒体给孩子们造成的消极影响 ········· *51*
3. 提高脑和自主神经系统功能的方法 ··············· *53*
4. 公园运动器材的意义和作用 ····················· *54*
   (1) 滑梯 ····································· *55*
   (2) 秋千 ····································· *55*
   (3) 云梯 ····································· *56*
   (4) 造型运动器材和恐龙运动器材 ··············· *56*
   (5) 模拟爬树的运动器材 ······················· *56*
5. 公园运动器材与运动能力的增强 ················· *57*
   (1) 10 大体力 ································ *57*
   (2) 4 种基本的运动技能 ······················· *58*
   (3) 运动时培养的能力 ························· *59*
6. 关于公园运动器材基本的安全管理及使用方法 ······ *60*

Part Ⅱ (English)

Daily rhythm improvement strategy: Encouraging the "Eat, be active and sleep well" movement 65

1. Three problems faced by children in recent years 65
   (1) Sleep rhythm out of order 65
   (2) Eating rhythm out of order 66
   (3) Lack of exercise 67
2. Body temperature rhythm affected by autonomic nerves and hormones in the brain 68
3. Launch of the "Go to bed early, get up early and have breakfast" movement and challenges 71
4. The importance in meeting new challenges 73

Why are physical activities during young childhood so important? 74

1. The problem is not just about physical activities 74
2. Impressing experience forms "Liking" 76
3. It will even help enough just by watching over 77
4. Society, life cycle, and children's bodies correspondingly coaching to the various changes 78

Suggestions for physical education instruction methods for young children ·································· *80*

Introduction ·· *80*

Noteworthy points on physical education instructions
    for young children ·· *80*

1. Noteworthy points at the introductory scene ····················· *80*
   (1) Safe environmental setting ·· *80*
   (2) Clothing ·· *81*
   (3) Teacher's standing position ······································· *82*
   (4) Formation ·· *83*
   (5) Alignment・distance to children ································ *84*
   (6) Warm-up ··· *85*
   (7) Grouping ··· *86*

2. Noteworthy points in the development scene ····················· *86*
   (1) Manner of speaking ·· *86*
   (2) Consideration for the fearsome child ··························· *86*
   (3) Momentum ··· *87*
   (4) Assistance ·· *87*
   (5) Mastering skills ·· *87*
   (6) Sustained concentration ·· *88*
   (7) The making of a pleasant atmosphere ·························· *89*
   (8) Feeling of satisfaction ·· *90*
   (9) Stirring up motivation ··· *90*
   (10) Fostering independence, spontaneity and creativity ········ *91*

(11) Response to danger 91
(12) Competition 92
3. Ending scene 93
   (1) Cooling down exercise 93
   (2) Clearing 93
   (3) Summary of the activity 94
   (4) Security after the exercise and hygiene 94

Park play equipment and raising children 96
Introduction 96
1. Health management problems held by children
   in recent years 97
   (1) Negative influence on children by pursuing an adult
       nightlife 97
   (2) Negative impact of excessive media contact on children 100
2. How to increase the work of children's brain and
   autonomic nerves 103
3. Significance and role of park play equipment 104
   (1) Slide stand 105
   (2) Swing 106
   (3) Monkey bars 106
   (4) Monument playground equipment • dinosaur play
       equipment 106
   (5) Tree climbing playground equipment 107

4. Ability to be cultivated with park playground equipment ··· *108*
  (1) 10 physical fitness factors ·· *108*
  (2) basic movement skills ·· *110*
  (3) Ability to grow during exercise ······································ *111*
  (4) Safety management (basic) of park playground
     equipment and safe usage ··· *112*

Children's health and welfare strategy in Japan ············· *116*
  POINT1: Propagation of the theory of recent children's
          problem appearance ······································ *116*
  POINT 2: Proposal of 3033 practice ····························· *118*
  POINT 3: Spreading of family exercise ························· *119*

Part Ⅲ (PPT)

婴幼儿健康生活的重要性－饮食、运动以及充足睡眠－ ⋯ *123*

游戏运动与促进幼儿身心发展－婴幼儿体力提升－ ⋯⋯⋯ *146*

幼儿体育是什么－从运动产生的生理机制来看－ ⋯⋯⋯ *157*

幼儿体育指导上的注意事项 ⋯⋯⋯⋯⋯⋯⋯⋯⋯⋯⋯⋯ *161*

「吃、动、充足睡眠！」运动的目的
－孩子成长发育的诊断与评价－ ⋯⋯⋯⋯⋯⋯⋯⋯⋯⋯ *193*

公园内运动器材的重要性 ⋯⋯⋯⋯⋯⋯⋯⋯⋯⋯⋯⋯⋯ *211*

前桥 明教授的简介 ⋯⋯⋯⋯⋯⋯⋯⋯⋯⋯⋯⋯⋯⋯⋯ *240*

Part I

生活作息对幼儿健康的重要性
― "吃好、睡好、运动好"的运动策略 ―

在日本，孩子们学习能力和体力低下、心理问题等的增加已经成为一个社会问题，需要幼儿园和学校、家庭、社区一同携手解决。我们认为，要想为培养身心健全的孩子贡献力量，首先，要对孩子们的生活状况或体力、运动能力进行测查，同时由行政机关或保育、教育机关、社会团体等共同携手，来发现孩子们心理和身体上的问题、分析问题并提出对策。我们根据各个地区的特征，在为孩子的健康做努力也在做幼儿运动的实操指导（亲子互动体操指导）。

在此，我们从近年来孩子生活中所存在的问题谈起，从以下3点开始进行介绍。

1．近年来幼儿所面临的三个问题

（1） 睡眠节奏不规律

首先，我们注意到现在的孩子们，有很多被带入大人们的夜晚型生活。大街上随处可以看到"吃好、喝好、玩好"这样的酒馆看板。我们也常看到父母深夜还带着幼儿出入家庭餐厅、居酒

屋（日式小酒馆）以及卡拉OK的包厢等。这些家长们对此说法是"没关系，孩子还很精神"、"因为晚上才有父子沟通的时间"、"孩子自己说不困不想睡"，因此幼儿深夜未眠的家庭逐渐增加。幼儿的生活就陷入"晚睡晚起、筋疲力尽"的状态。

另外，为了成人健身，有些中小学体育馆是在夜间开放的，有的大人带着孩子一直待到夜里9至10点，大人们既能运动又能互相交流非常地尽兴。孩子们要等着父母运动完后再吃晚饭的例子非常多。孩子们被卷入大人们的夜晚型生活而陷入不健康的生活状态，父母不知道孩子的健康生活作息应该是什么样的，缺乏大人的生活作息要符合孩子这样的知识和意识，这样的种种现象非常明显。

在生活实际状况调查中，平成10（1998）年的全国性调查结果显示，在日本晚上10点以后才入睡的孩子占40%（厚生省报告）。前桥明研究室平成17（2005）年的调查结果指出，有些地区10点后入睡孩子的比例已经超过了50%，例如高知县土佐山田町和冲绳县石垣市（石垣岛）的孩子们。另外，平成18（2006）年的调查结果也显示，自然环境丰富的高知县仁淀川町的幼儿超过50%的都是晚间10点以后才入睡。此后，平成19（2007）年的调查结果来看，冲绳县那霸市的幼儿晚睡率达到68.5%，西日本的大城市大阪也高达49.6%。在这样的情况下，很难期待孩子能有良好的学力和体力。

从小睡眠就有问题的孩子进入小学后，在学习上很难达到优秀。睡眠的作用，不仅能恢复疲劳，而且在睡眠中把我们每天看到和听到的信息在大脑中进行整理，并做为记忆固定下来。也

就是说，睡眠和学力是有关联的。睡眠能保护我们的大脑，所以乳幼儿期的睡眠很重要。

昭和50年代（20世纪70,80年代）的孩子们，不只是幼儿，小学生也在晚上8点左右就睡了。"过了晚上8点是大人们的时间"这句话在日本也耳熟能详。在此，需要我们思考的是，幼儿园、小学开始上课的时间从那时到现在是没有改变过的。也就是说，与以前相比早上学校开始的时间没有变，但是晚睡2个小时的孩子却增多了。这样一来就会造成睡眠不足，或者为了保证睡眠出现晚起的现象，早上的时间也就变得很紧张。

（2）饮食节奏的混乱

如果不吃早饭孩子就会变得烦躁不安。幼儿就会出现乱扔积木、乱扔玩具、从后面推其他小朋友的现象。现在约8成的孩子吃早饭，而另外2成的孩子没有吃早饭，我们把这部分不吃早饭的现象称做为不规律饮食。

我们大人每天吃早、午、晚三餐维持生活，而幼儿处于快速成长期，只靠一日三餐是不够的。并且幼儿胃小、肠蠕动较弱，所以一次不能足够摄取身体所需要的食物，若摄取过多也不易消化、也不易吸收，所以必须加餐以补充其摄入不足。因此，点心之类的也应考虑列为每天用餐的一部分。也就是说，对幼儿而言，每天必须吃4～5顿。尽管如此，缺少主要一餐（早餐）的幼儿的不断增加是十分令人担心的。小学生也出现同样的情况，即吃完早饭才去学校的孩子也只占8成左右。

另外，还有更令人担心的问题。例如，6岁的幼儿虽有80%

左右吃早餐,但是,有早上排便习惯的幼儿只有21%左右。人类吃进食物,如果是容易消化的食物,约7小时左右的时间就会变成粪便。若是需要好好地消化干净则将花费24小时左右的时间。如果晚上约10点左右入睡,晚餐所摄取食物当中消化良好的食物残渣,第二天清晨就已经到达大肠。早上的胃是空空的,早餐吃进的食物进入胃时,胃就会将此信息传达到脑部。为了将大肠内的残渣排出体外,脑传命令给大肠,大肠开始蠕动将残渣排出体外。大肠内积满食物残渣是非常重要的,如果不好好吃饭只吃零食的话,肠内就不会有相当重量和体积的食物残渣,也就是说如果不吃高质量的食物是不能达到良好排便的。

在一些调查中,有些孩子明明没有吃早饭,有些家长却也谎称说是吃了。但是关于孩子的排便问题,家长们都很如实地回答。因为家长并没有意识到孩子早上没有排便有多么不好。现在,早上不排便就入园或入校的孩子很多,这些孩子大多很难走出家门或身体上不是很舒服,因此上午的活动能力低下可想而知。如果不怎么动的话,1天的运动量就有所减少体力得不到提高。

(3) 运动不足

我们关心的第三个问题,是幼儿在生活当中,运动量急剧减少的问题,例如,保育园5岁的幼儿,昭和60～62(1985-1987)年,从上午9点到下午4点之间,走路活动步数约为1万2千步,但是,到平成3～5(1991-1993)年时,减少到7千至8千步。然而,到了平成10(1998)年以后,大量减少到5千步。现如今,幼儿的步行数已经减少到只占昭和时代的一半左右。而目前

因利用以车代步，送幼儿入园的家长人数逐渐增加，在幼儿的生活中整体上步行数减少，必要的运动量不足。

观察幼儿活动时的样子，过圆木或平衡木时，有因脚趾翘起不能保持平衡而掉落下来的孩子。如果在生活中没有充分行走的话，是保持不了平衡的。跑的时候也同样，会有因膝盖不能抬起而造成指尖拖地的现象。

另外，幼儿通常都在室内看电视、打电动游戏以及看 DVD 等，很少进行户外游戏，所以对活动场所的距离感、人与人之间距离感的认知能力（空间认知能力）得不到培养，因此撞到人的情况很多。因为日常生活的运动不足，当因碰撞而差点摔倒的时候，也不会做自我保护动作而导致自己的脸部着地受伤。

2．休息、营养、运动问题的出现与自主神经系统

孩子们的睡眠节奏若混乱，就不能很好地用餐，发生少餐或没有排便的问题。结果会导致上午的活动能力低下不想动。并且，如果睡眠节奏混乱或少餐、运动不足，自动保护我们身体的脑或自主神经系统功能就变得低下，依自主神经系统进行的体温调节功能就不能很好地进行，体温无法保持在 36.0℃至 36.9℃之间。不能调节体温的"高体温"和"低体温"的幼儿，因体温变化脱离正常范围，就会造成他们早上体温低不想动，晚上体温升高且没有睡意。

因此，了解了体温的变化规律，我们就会理解育儿或教育中好多的事。我们在这里介绍一下关于体温的知识。

3．体温的变化规律

（1） 随着年龄增长体温的变化规律也不同

乳幼儿期体温的调节功能还没有发育成熟，所以体温的变动易受外部环境的影响。一般情况下，新生儿出生后3天内体温是比较高的，随后逐渐下降，过了100天后体温降至37℃以下，到了120天左右就逐渐稳定下来。另外，从2至3岁左右开始，体温在1日内的变动范围大概是0.6至1.0℃左右。在日常生活中，体温一般在凌晨3点左右处于最低值，午后4点左右处于最高值，人的体温就是处于这样一个循环变化中，这是经过漫长时间的衍变而形成的一种生物钟。午后4点左右也就是孩子们的放学时间，对于孩子来说是个运动的"黄金时间"。

但是，晚睡晚起孩子的体温变化与正常体温变化规律有所出入，大概相差几个小时左右。晚睡晚起孩子的体温在早上还是一个入睡状态时的体温，此时让他起床开始进行活动的话，就会睁不开眼动作变得迟钝。相反，到了夜里体温很高怎么也不能入睡，就会造成一个恶性循环。使体温节奏重新回归正常，我们介绍两点有效方法，①早晨能让孩子晒到太阳，②白天让幼儿多进行运动。

（2） 低体温对身体的影响

早上起床时处于低体温状态，说明身体还没有进入活动状态，脑也处于没觉醒而不得不进行活动的状态。所以，即使让

他们进行活动，也会表现得没有力气和精神，所以学习的东西做不好也记不住。也就是身体不能很好地进行预热。加之，不吃早饭、白天运动不足、身体散热少的话，自主神经系统就得不到锻炼，体温就不能被很好地控制，夜里的睡眠质量也不会好。

（3） 改善体温变化的方法

要改善体温变化，做到"早睡早起（改善生活作息）"是根本。在现如今的日本，晚上 10 点后入睡的幼儿超过 4 成左右，可谓是一个国家性危机。需要从幼儿期意识到以"睡眠"为基础的"塑造孩子健康生活习惯的重要性"。

作为解决夜晚型孩子起床与不吃早饭问题的具体对策，要让孩子早睡 1 个小时。据此，能让孩子吃好早饭并有早便拥有原本应有的生活节奏，同时也能保证孩子在入园后能有良好的情绪与人际关系。也就是说，为了改善孩子的生活作息就要"把入睡时间提前"，为此首先要做到吃早饭并保证白天的运动。这也对提高体温调节自主神经系统的功能有作用。

其中，白天在阳光下做户外运动，能使孩子们的体温上升，出汗并使身体放热，提高自主神经系统的功能。尤其是"增加下午户外活动的时间或运动量让孩子酣畅淋漓"，"不让孩子晚睡看电视，让孩子健康地使用电视手机"，这些对于改善孩子的生活作息十分有效。

（4）体内生物钟与脑内荷尔蒙

人为了保证夜里睡眠早上起来进行多种多样的活动，荷尔蒙的作用非常的重要。夜晚分泌褪黑色素以便于睡眠，早上开始分泌皮质醇以保证精力充沛，如果缺乏这样激素的分泌，孩子就不能好好地睡眠与活动。如果这些激素分泌时间或量产生紊乱的话，脑内的温度就得不到调节，脑内状况就如倒时差一样，无论做什么都打不起精神来。在健康的状况下，促进睡眠的褪黑色素的分泌，在凌晨12点左右达到高峰值，此后脑内的温度开始下降。因此，神经细胞得以恢复，孩子们才会有良好的睡眠。

（5）午睡的作用

上午孩子们沉浸于活动当中脑内温度不断升高，容易陷入脑内温度过热的情况。为了防止这种现象的出现，需要有能够让大脑休息的午睡。虽然说孩子的体力有所提高，即便是不睡午觉也可以，但是对于大脑功能还比较弱的孩子来说，一时地让脑内温度降下来恢复到通常的体温，也就是通过午睡让孩子的大脑休息非常的必要。如果没有午睡的话体力低下的孩子就调节不了脑内的温度。如果不让孩子午睡那么白天的睡眠时间就相对减少，夜里似乎可以早睡，但是因为幼儿的大脑发育还未成熟，不能把温度降下来，长此以往就会导致自主神经功能低下或荷尔蒙分泌混乱。

因此，年龄较小的幼儿在上午活动过程中上升起来的体温，要通过午睡让其降下来，这非常的重要。对于体力比较好的孩子来说，可以不勉强他睡，但是需要确保给孩子创造一个让大脑能

够休息的"静的时间"。

4．睡眠进一步混乱带来的问题

睡眠节奏的进一步混乱，体内生物钟就会紊乱，荷尔蒙的分泌也会紊乱，有助于睡眠的褪黑色素和有助于白天活动的皮质醇分泌的时间就会错位，体温调节就会更加的不好。结果夜里脑内的温度会降不下来，神经细胞的休息不够睡眠时间变长。因此就会造成早上起不来、晚上睡不够的情况。这样的话，早上起不来到了下午皮质醇终于开始分泌，孩子稍微能够打起精神来了。当然能力会是极度低下的，结果就会造成易疲劳耐力低下、注意力不集中、脑子混沌、烦躁不安、没有力气或是处于抑郁状态。

另外，近些年来孩子们从幼儿期开始就学习多种多样的技能并且种类增加，因此大脑需要处理的信息量有所增加，而与此相比睡眠时间（睡眠不足）在减少，疲劳难以得到消解能力极度低下。并且，将来进入初高中也不能集中注意力、学不进东西，日常生活变得困难整天待在家里。

5．创造健康生活的建议

为了让孩子提早入睡，"在孩子的日常生活中，让他们在阳光下多做户外运动"，"增加午后的运动时间与运动量，让其酣畅淋漓地运动"，并且"努力缩短孩子看电视的时间，也不要让孩子看电视看到很晚"，这些方法比较有效。但是仅从电子媒体

（电视、手机）的使用方法上下功夫解决不了根本问题。也就是说，从幼少儿时期开始必须要孩子体验到运动的乐趣，这种乐趣是不输给电子媒体的、来自于与人进行交流的运动游戏或体育项目的乐趣。

解决孩子学力与体力的问题的关键在于以下三要素，①每天的饮食、②运动量、③交流体验。首先让孩子吃早饭，并且有充足的能与人交流的运动游戏或体育活动的体验。为了能让这种体验感动孩子，我们需要在指导上多加努力多下功夫。

为了孩子的身体和心理的健康，要让小学低年级学生在晚上9点前，小学高年级学生在9点半以前入睡。入睡时间很晚的话就会出现很多的状况是非常令人担心的。会诱发不能集中注意力、烦躁不安、易激惹、夜晚徘徊、自主神经系统功能低下、干什么事都没有兴趣等症状，诱发生活习惯病。

6．近年来孩子们所存在的问题

如果睡眠节奏混乱、运动不足、饮食不规律、皮质醇的分泌时间就会错位。另外，早晨叫醒我们的皮质醇得不到分泌的话就起不来床。也就是说我们的大脑还在处于睡眠状态，白天就喜欢呆在家里，不想去学校。

提高脑内温度让我们打起精神的荷尔蒙，由于分泌时间的错位到了晚上才开始分泌，夜里才达到最高值。换句话说，早上起不来床夜里睡不踏实，陷入这样的一个生活状态。

总之，睡眠节奏混乱就会吃不上早饭，饮食节奏也跟着混

乱。摄取不到能量，上午的活动能力低下，继而造成运动不足。并且，自主神经系统的功能减弱，体温变化节奏混乱，随之不久荷尔蒙分泌节奏也就开始混乱。如果陷入这种状态的话，孩子们就会身体不适精神不安，不能进行学习。学力和体力低下引起心理上的问题。

也就是说，孩子的睡眠、饮食、运动得不到保障的话，自主神经系统的功能就会减弱，不能自动地进行调节来保护我们的身体。没有做事的兴趣，不能自发和自主地进行多种多样的活动。教育中经常讲的"有活力"就是医学和生理学中所说的"自主神经系统功能"。大人们务必要重视孩子的"睡眠"、"饮食"、"运动"。如果自主神经系统的功能低下，我们要考虑运动疗法。这个运动疗法不是命令让孩子做某一项运动，是让孩子有做运动的欲望。因为孩子自主神经系统功能低下的话，就没有运动的欲望。让孩子散步或者活动一下身体，孩子就容易饿食欲好，并且也容易睡好觉。

为了防止孩子们活动力和体力低下，关于睡眠和饮食这一方面需要家长的配合。同时，怎样对待活动力低下的孩子、怎样在保育与教育实践中改善他们的状况、得到更好的教育效果，对于这些问题，幼儿园和学校所做的努力和研究很重要。

因此，在日本倡导"早睡、早起、吃早饭"的国民运动。如图1所示。日本孩子们的问题是怎样出现的呢，我们来分析一下它产生的一系列流程。为了解决学力低下的问题，首先需要解决"睡眠"的问题，也就是"早睡、早起"。

接下来，如果睡眠出了问题那么"饮食"就会出现问题，也

```
睡眠节奏混乱
      ↓
饮食节奏混乱（不吃早餐）
      ↓
上午的活动力低下、1天的运动量减少（运动能力不足、体力下降）
      ↓
自动调节保护身体的自主神经系统技能低下
（昼夜体温变化失调、不能进行自发地、自主性地运动）
      ↓
荷尔蒙分泌节奏不规律
（早上赖床起不来、白天活动不了、晚上无法睡好）
      ↓
容易造成身体不适、精神状态不稳定
      ↓
学力低下、体力低下、不上学、暴力行为
```

图 1　日本幼儿的现存问题及其产生的连锁关系

就是"早饭"。这个国民运动只考虑到这一步。如果希望孩子有能够自发自主地进行活动并且能思考的话，那么第 3 点的"运动"刺激在生活中不可缺少。运动和运动游戏对自主神经系统的发展不可或缺。也就是说，不提高自主神经系统的功能的话，就不能使孩子能够自发地投入到学习中。因此，在"早睡、早起，吃早饭"中不加入"运动"的话，是有所欠缺的。

也就是说，"吃好"、"睡好"、"运动好"，务必要加入运动在里面。我们希望以此来构建孩子们的健康生活，让他们担当起未来。

7．培养孩子健康全面发展的目标

以孩子为对象,通过各种游戏与活动、指导等来谋求他们成为真正的社会人。也就是说,把它放在企求孩子全面发展的教育整体当中。

这个全面发展是指,身体的（physical）、社会的（social）、智力的（intellectual）、精神的（spiritual）、情绪的（emotional）的发展。

8．孩子的成长、发展状况的诊断和评价

(1) 睡眠·休养

作为人们生活基本的睡眠,不仅是睡眠的长短,睡觉的时间和起床的时间也很重要。早上起来的时候,不留有前一天的疲惫, 清清爽爽地起床是非常重要的。

- 晚上尽量在9点之前睡吗?
- 每天晚上都能睡10小时以上吗?
- 早上7点之前能起床吗?
- 早上起床的时候能沐浴到阳光吗?
- 早上起来的时候很精神吗?

（2） 营养·膳食

就餐对于塑造健康的身体来说必不可少，家人或朋友在一起吃饭的团圆之乐，能成为孩子心理上的营养补给。为了能让孩子每天吃饭吃得很香，大人们有在努力做些什么吗？

- 每天吃早饭吗？
- 早上都有排便吗？
- 能开开心心地吃饭吗？
- 吃完零食到晚饭之间有 2 个小时左右的间隔吗？
- 努力不让孩子吃夜宵吗？

（3） 活 动

除了睡眠、就餐以外，我们挑选了一些主要活动。即便是做帮手或看电视这样的小事，做为生活习惯反复的持续下去的话，其影响是不容忽视的。

- 徒步去幼儿园吗？
- 在户外，能玩得出汗吗？
- 能够为运动身体努力做些什么吗？
- 看电视玩游戏的时间，合起来在 1 个小时之内吗？
- 晚上，能够悠闲地泡澡吗？

（4） 运动之基本

现状下能对孩子在外的运动量和运动能力有所把握吗？如果不确定，可以和孩子去公园一起试着做一下，看看孩子们能达到一个什么水平。

- 上午在室外玩耍呢吗？
- 15～17点间是否在户外玩耍？
- 比例均衡地在做跑、跳、投球等运动吗？
- 能够在单杠和云梯等下面做悬垂，在平衡木上能保持平衡之类的吗？
- 能够享受到玩幼儿园户外或公园的固定游具的乐趣吗？

（5） 发展的均衡性

（身体的 · 社会的 · 智力的 · 精神的 · 情绪的发展）

是否有保护自己身体的体力、能否和他人建立良好的关系、是否能够在玩儿上下功夫、是否有努力到最后的实力、是否有忍耐的精神等，我们可以确认一下这些在游戏过程能被培养出来的多种多样的能力。幼儿期孩子的生活因家长精力的倾注和同家长的关系的不同会有很大的不一样。

- 当孩子摔倒的时候，能收起下颌用手掌着地来保护身体吗？（身体的 · 自我保护的能力）
- 能和朋友一起和和乐乐地玩耍吗？（社会的）
- 能够在游戏的玩法上下功夫，开心地玩耍吗？（智力的）
- 玩耍完之后整理东西能坚持到最后吗？（精神的）
- 即使是和人发生碰撞，能够控制自己的情绪吗？（情绪的）

（6）父母的作用和帮助

- 有在努力创造进行亲子活动的机会吗？
- 注重在户外玩耍（家周围或公园等）的机会吗？
- 比起坐车，有坚持陪孩子一起走步出行吗？
- 有和孩子随着音乐一起跳舞或做体操、做手指操吗？
- 有在努力让孩子1天做30分种以上的运动吗？

9．现如今，如果您都厌倦了，那么孩子会变得很糟糕

孩子在晚上的睡眠期间，分泌能够降低脑内温度让身体休息的叫作"褪黑色素"的激素和有助于成长发育和细胞新生的激素。现如今，受成人夜晚型生活的影响，孩子体内生物钟被打乱。不规则的生活节奏会导致孩子无缘无故地发脾气、烦躁不安、精神不集中、人际关系不好、感觉没有精神等等问题。生活节奏不规律，孩子的身体会出现问题，对心理也会带来不好的影响。

这些问题的改善,归根结底来说,大人们更加认真地重视"乳幼儿期孩子应有的生活"是很必要的。调整好生活习惯的基础之上，也要在一日生活当中，给孩子提供释放运动能量、获得情绪解放的机会和场所，不要错看降低脑内温度、避免脑内温度过于升高的午睡或让他们安静下来的时间的重要性。因此，首先一天当中的运动游戏显得是非常重要。

运动、运动游戏，增强孩子体力的活动毋庸置疑会对促进基

础代谢和体温调节、或者是对促进脑和神经的活动都起着重要的作用。在园所和学校、社区如果能给孩子们提供一个能够尽兴玩耍的环境,孩子们就能够顺顺利利地成长下去。总结为就是,①早上要吃饭、②白天要运动、③要带着酣畅淋漓地疲累早睡,这几项非常重要。也就是说"吃、动、睡好觉!"。

幼儿体育的意义与作用

1. 幼儿体育的定义

如果把幼儿的"体育"从"通过身体活动对幼儿进行教育"角度来理解的话，那么，幼儿体育就是指为了让孩子在身体上、社会上、智力上、精神上、情绪上的各个层面得到均衡发展，通过多种多样的身体活动（活动游戏、运动游戏、模仿类游戏、音乐律动、舞蹈等）来进行教育。目的是为了培养身心全面发展的社会人。

另外，体育既然是教育，那么在其实施的过程中讲究系统化和结构化是非常必要的。也就是说，把握成为教育对象的"幼儿"的实际状况，制定指导目标，使学习内容结构化，寻找好的指导方法并进行教学效果的评价，把评价做为今后的教学资料，这种种事项都很必要。同时，幼儿体育是以运动或运动游戏为主进行的，保证健康安全地进行不可或缺。

2. 幼儿体育的目标

对于幼儿期体育指导来说最重要的，不是以通过运动来提升孩子的体力与运动技能为主要目的，而是必须优先考虑让孩子"有什么样的心动体验了？"，"心情是什么样的？"等"心动"的体验。也就是说，为了"育心"而"育体"。

另外，针对于目前孩子们的现状，幼儿体育要以以下3点为目的。

①培养孩子自己发现、思考与判断，进行问题解决的积极性和相应的意志力。
②培养孩子同他人合作，关心同伴以及怀有感恩之心等等的社会性。
③让孩子掌握运动技能和具备能够健健康康生活的体力等，并提高孩子的运动能力。

3. 幼儿体育的指导方法

幼儿体育指导首先是依指导老师对孩子的理解来开展的。因此，从中会反映出指导老师自身的个性与经验，依据幼儿的不同，指导方法等有所不同是很正常的。

(1) 指导方法

首先在指导者有目的地对孩子实施教育的过程中,①直接示范而进行指导(教养上的目标)。这类指导由指导老师把一些包含了价值观的内容直接向孩子进行示范。特别是关于运动规则或安全上的一些规定居多。依此,孩子们的活动会变得容易一些。但是根据内容和具体情况,也要让孩子自己去思考、去选择哪一个合适或怎样进行组合。

其次,②是让孩子们自己去思考的指导类型。这种指导与直接示范型相对应,多用在当孩子出现了不被期许的行为时。依据这个指导,不是由指导老师单方面地去示范行为的好坏,而是让孩子把运动课题当做孩子自己的事情积极地去对待。

(2) 指导技巧

关于指导的技巧,首先可以列举的是"确认孩子做出的我们所期许的动作后,告知其他的孩子们"这样的方法。对于做出期许动作的孩子"○○,真了不起呀!","○○好快呀,大家给他鼓掌!""有些小朋友坐得很好,在认真地听老师的话呢!"等等,用这些言语来肯定做得好的孩子并让其他孩子知道。

对于孩子出现了不被期许的行为,也不要直接地指出错误,要采用非常委婉的方法给孩子做示范。这样委婉的方法可以让小孩子在加快速度或活动时使用,如"女孩子要快点儿了","10,9,8,7……","○○比较快哟"等表现。另外,也有"利用表情或态度进行示范"的非言语性指导。孩子们能够从指导老师的表情和态度来感受到价值观的所在从而判断善恶。对于孩子们来

说，得到自己所喜欢的指导老师的肯定并产生共鸣，能直接地起到指导的作用，也能间接地引发孩子的积极性。另一方面，对那些不被期许的行为不仅要以语言也要以态度进行回应。也就是说，在多种情境下把需要孩子自己去思考或判断的东西以言语或非言语的方式明示出来。尤其是有一点不能忘记"指导老师自身就能够引起孩子的注意"，指导老师自身的存在就会影响孩子的活动。也就是说，唯有指导老师的指导才会让孩子对活动产生兴趣，才能和老师一起有所行动。

总之，幼儿体育指导老师有必要帮助每个孩子获得成功，也需要如做榜样或做示范等这些丰富多样的指导技巧。

4．需要让孩子们体验的运动

对照近年来幼儿身体和生活的实际状况，介绍以下对于日本幼儿来说所必需的运动内容。其中包括培养颠倒和旋转感的倒立或旋转运动，保持平衡与反应能力的四散跑或球类运动，培养空间认知能力的"爬"、"钻"、"转"、"登"等基本的运动。另外，也需要重视能够锻炼孩子自主神经系统、培养五感，促进身体机能发展的户外运动及游戏。

- 尽可能多的运动种类
- 多体验如倒立、旋转等日常生活中较少体验到的运动
- 培养颠倒感、旋转感、节奏感、灵活性、柔韧性以及耐力的运动
- 亲近大自然的活动，特别是登山、越过小溪等等的运动

- 提高反应能力、培养躲避危险能力的运动
- 支撑自身身体的运动
- 全身心地投入到四散跑活动
- 能够充分地表现自己的韵律表现活动
- 培养操作绳子以及球类能力的运动
- 与机械运动相互关联的运动

5．对幼儿体育的期待

- 不仅仅是在技能方面，更要充分地考虑孩子的发展把目标指向"社会人的形成"。
- 比起提高孩子的技术，可把焦点放在扩大孩子的擅长项目的种类上。
- 在愉悦的气氛当中，体验多种多样的活动。
- 不要勉强孩子，要尽可能地符合孩子的兴趣以比较自然的方式为孩子提供多种多样的运动情景。
- 不要只要求技术方面，也要重视培养孩子友好的、相互合作的、守规矩的心理层面。
- 目标是让孩子体验运动的快乐与培养孩子的灵巧性。

6．幼儿体育应有的状态

- 不仅仅是让孩子进行特定的运动得到技术层面的提升，更需要通过多种多样的运动游戏体验来让孩子亲近运动。
- 即便是不擅长，也要通过多种多样的运动让孩子来体验到玩耍的快乐之处，培养能够开开心心地进行运动的孩子。
- 让孩子们精神饱满、活力十足地进行运动，从中也要让孩子们体会到运动的快乐与乐趣。
- 把提高能够灵巧地运用身体的"调整能力"做为重点。
- 孩子对于感觉方面的体验从很小的时候就能够掌握的，所以可以从幼儿期开始就对孩子进行旋转感或颠倒感的指导。
- 让孩子通过游戏培养出属于自己的创造性并能够有助于其它活动的进行。
- 对于幼儿期的孩子们来说，不要留给他们过难的任务，让他们更多地进行跑、跳、旋转，同时在户外更多地去接触自然。
- 增加孩子们户外（大自然）运动的经验。
- 做为健康生活的构成要素，要认识运动的重要性以及将运动付诸实践。
- 了解均衡饮食的基础知识。
- 了解主要的身体部位或各器官的功能、位置和正确的身体姿势。
- 要热衷于运动游戏，从中得到快乐与满足等。

7．进行幼儿体育指导时的注意事项

（1）确保足够的空间，确认周围没有其他人和事物的干扰，确认安全之后再进行。而且关于安全的条约准则、注意事项等，要在活动开始之前告知孩子们。如果孩子们的着装不整，为了安全考虑也要整理好之后再进行。

（2）对怀有胆怯心理的孩子，不要勉强他们。另外对于做不到的孩子要帮助他们努力完成，并用言语好好地去鼓励他们。

（3）对于指导老师们来说，说话要能引起孩子们的兴趣，以及运用孩子们易懂的教学语言。而且说话的时候，眼睛要看着孩子。

（4）指导者们给孩子做示范的时候要做到精神饱满地、大幅度地、通俗易懂地进行示范。这样的话，孩子们才更有兴趣去做。但是，孩子们也会模仿大人们不好的地方。所以在做示范的时候，一定要用正确的、标准的动作。特别是应该伸展的地方要好好伸展，应该弯曲的地方要好好弯曲。

（5）用笑脸来营造轻松活跃的气氛，让孩子们感受到快乐，这是十分重要的。而且指导老师们也要一起参与，用心去体会活动的乐趣与快乐，与孩子们产生共鸣。

（6）让孩子们感受到大人身体的高大和力量的强大是很重要的。孩子切实地感受到大人力量的强大，可以使孩子更加信赖大人，不过要注意控制力量。

（7）简单而又能让身体得到充分活动的动作比较好。来试着改

变运动方向，时而上下活动身体，时而扭转一下身体。

（8）天气寒冷的时候，为了让身体暖和起来，多做一些活动量大的活动。

（9）学习内容一般是由简单到复杂，通过慢慢地增加难度来设置。但有些时候，选择一个难的学习内容，以适当地带给孩子们紧张感，对于能更好地让孩子集中注意力，保持好奇心是非常重要的。

（10）当发现孩子经过努力很好地完成动作时要好好地表扬孩子，给予孩子教育意义上的优越感。

（11）虽然教孩子如何去做使他们变得更好很重要，但是给孩子时间让孩子自己去思考解决对策也很重要。

（12）对于孩子们不懂的地方，老师们要亲自地进行示范手把手地教，这会让孩子们理解起来更容易。

（13）对于努力去做的孩子老师们也要很好的去回应。不管是已经做得很好，或是努力争取的时候，还是煞费苦心的时候，老师们都要好好地去表扬孩子。这么一来，可以让孩子们充满积极性，并因获得表扬而拥有更多的自信心。

（14）告知孩子们，利用日常生活中的物品或废旧物品，也能玩得很好。

幼儿体育需要了解的重点内容

关于幼儿体育，想要大家了解的关于理论与实践的重点内容共21项，列举如下。

1．幼儿体育的理论方面

(1) 近些年可以看到入园之后不去玩耍而一动不动的孩子们，以及许多注意力不集中的孩子们，他们的体温特征都被确认为被控制到36度范围之内。孩子们的体温调节出现了问题，是由于自主神经系统的功能无法很好地进行而造成的。我们试着分析了孩子们生活的实际状况，可以看出这些孩子有一些共同点，那就是生活习惯和睡眠节奏出现了问题，即运动不足、睡眠不足、不吃早饭，在被设置好温度的室内过多地接触电子媒体进行娱乐。总之，对于孩子们来说，让他们迎合太阳来生活，在白天可以让他们一边沐浴太阳光一边进行户外活动。在户外通过跑跳等等的活动无意之间就可以起到锻炼筋骨的目的，使体温上升，从而促进了荷尔蒙的分泌，使身体回归到正常的生活节奏。对于现在的孩子们来说，运动是绝对必要的。大人们要意识到这一点，积极地给孩子创

造运动的机会不可或缺。

(2) 如果孩子们的睡眠节奏被打乱,就会出现饮食不规律、不吃早饭、不排便等情况。于是上午孩子们的活动能力变得低下、运动不足,从而导致自主神经功能低下、昼夜体温变化紊乱、荷尔蒙的分泌紊乱,造成孩子的身体不适、情绪不稳定等,长此以往就会导致孩子学习能力低下、体力低下、身心方面出现问题。诸如上述那样的孩子越来越多。为了防止这类事件的发生,我们要彻彻底底地从孩子们的幼儿时期就开始调整他们的生活习惯。

在调整孩子生活习惯的基础之上,在孩子们的1日生活当中,也不能忽视通过运动给孩子们提供能够散发能量、释放情绪的机会。为此,在幼儿期,每日的运动是非常非常重要的。特别是通过运动可以帮助优化孩子们自主神经系统的功能,让自主神经系统能够保护孩子身体的同时,也能让提高孩子们参与活动的积极性。

(3) 不同年龄段的孩子们一起玩耍的机会少了,孩子们与同伴之间的相互学习交流的体验就欠缺了。所以现如今的孩子们,如果没有机会把一些东西交给同伴,那他们也就失去了学以致用的机会。幼儿园的老师们要成为孩子的范本,必须给予孩子提供观看学习运动技能或进行动作示范的机会。关于运动技能的学习,如果老师不给示范不和小孩子们一同进行的话,对于幼儿期的孩子们来说很难正确掌握。

另外,如将游戏的基本形式教给孩子们,做多种多样的指导非常的重要。同时了解幼儿期的身体发展特征也不可或缺。

幼儿年龄越小头部的比例就越大、四肢的比例也越小。重心在身体的最上部，会导致孩子们在运动的过程中因重心不稳而容易摔倒。而且身体的平衡机能也没有得到很好的发展，当孩子们朝前倾斜身体的时候，一时地难以保持平衡导致头朝下脸部着地而摔倒的危险性增大。

（4）婴幼儿运动机能的发育，以从使用粗大的肌肉进行的粗大运动开始逐渐向末梢部分过渡。首先，与身高相比孩子头的比例要大一些。新生儿是 4∶1，1 至 2 岁的孩子是 5∶1。所以，由于重心在上，孩子们容易出现跌倒的现象，也容易出现头部或者脸部受伤的情况。从发展阶段来看，孩子 4 至 6 月之间就可以翻身了、俯卧了，7 至 10 个月的时候可以坐起、爬，10 个月至 1 岁 3 个月的时候可以扶着东西站起来，之后便可以一个人行走并逐渐变得稳定。为将来的走、跳、投的这些基础运动能力打好基础，从幼儿期开始活动身体是极其重要的。

（5）幼儿体育是通过各种身体运动或者游戏活动、从教育角度对幼儿进行指导，满足他们的运动需求、获得情绪解放、使身体各机能得到均衡发展，并且要促进孩子精神、智力和社会性的发展，培养身心健康发展的社会人。

在孩子的运动过程当中，提高孩子的运动技能不是主要目的，通过让孩子活动自己的身体，为孩子打下能够终生身心健康地生活下去的基础才是最重要的。并且，运动游戏与体育活动虽然存在不同，但是幼儿体育，就是通过"运动游戏"达成一个教育的目的。为了这个目的，从智力的、精神的、

社会等方面进行考虑，把运动游戏做为教学素材来用，从这个意义上来说可以把运动游戏称之为"体育游戏"。

(6) 在活动身体的时候，要由大脑去判断"怎么做出动作"，先是由大脑把命令传达给肌肉，肌肉收缩便使运动和活动产生。传达命令给肌肉让身体活动的是神经。运动是由感受器捕捉到的感觉，经过脊髓、将刺激传输给大脑，大脑辨别这个刺激并进行判断，随后发出命令。命令再通过脊髓，传达到运动神经，引起肌肉的收缩形成了运动。这就是运动的产生机制。

在幼儿期的运动中所常见的基本的运动技能可分为移动类运动技能、平衡类运动技能、操作类运动技能、非移动类运动技能4类。通过反复练习，在大脑中形成的运动回路不断得到巩固最终使动作达到熟练的程度。这些运动技能是我们终生所进行的体育活动、体操或健身等的基础。

(7) 在孩子的周围环境中存在着很多危险隐患，造成危险或事故的原因我们可以归结出以下4点，①危险的环境，②危险的行为，③危险的身心状态，④危险的服装。

从户外场地中发生事故的例子来看，以第二种原因产生的危险行为居多，例如自我中心、冲动冒险的行为等等。为了防止事故的发生，在日常的游戏过程中及时发现孩子的危险行为进行当场随机应变的处理是很重要的。另外在确保自我保护能力还很低的幼儿安全的同时，要提高他们的自我保护能力，为此提高孩子的运动能力也是很重要的。

而且，为了让孩子能灵活地进行活动提高他们回避危险的

运动能力，同时选择运动性能较高的鞋子很重要。选择鞋子的条件：①选择适合于运动的材料以及形状等；②选择不妨碍运动的尺码，还有要掌握正确的穿鞋、脱鞋的方法，养成整理好鞋子的习惯，这些也是至关重要的。

（8）对于走路有一些障碍的孩子们来说，充分地行走或跑对他们很重要。行走这样的运动是全身运动，对于全身肌肉以及心肺功能的发展十分有效。可以考虑选择进行散步，或像捉妖怪等锻炼跑的游戏活动。一般对于走路有一些障碍的孩子来说，他们对摇晃的处于高处位置的运动比较恐惧，所以可以从诸如垫上运动或过平衡木这样的处于低处位置运动开始进行指导比较好。而且，通过使用各种游具来活动身体，在提高平衡感、注意力、身体认识等方面的效果也是值得期待的。

为了促进孩子手脚协调性的发展，可以将蹦床、平衡木、爬梯子等组合起来形成循环进行运动，特别的有效。循环运动，是按照事先规定好的循环路线——进行的，所以即使是低智商儿也能完成。这样也可以让孩子获得多种多样的运动体验，是为孩子创设运动环境的重要方法。

（9）所谓体力是孩子们为维持生命活动而进行必要的身体活动的能力，包括行动体力和防卫体力。行动体力就是使动作得以发生的能力（力量、爆发力）、使动作持续进行的能力（肌肉耐力、全身的耐力）、正确地完成动作的能力（敏捷性、平衡性、灵巧性、协调性）、动作得以顺利进行的能力（柔软性、节奏感、速度）。另外，防卫体力可分为体温调节能力、

免疫力等多种能够应对疲劳的抵抗力。所谓的运动能力是在运动时可以使运动很好地进行下去所需要的能力。

也就是说，体力就是发挥肌肉力量、耐力、柔韧性或敏捷性时所具备的排除机体障碍的能力。运动能力是像跑、跳、投这样在体力基础之上，加入运动或体育活动时所必需的基本动作技能这样意义在内的能力。

（10）下面是关于测量体力、运动能力时的注意的事项。首先，需清楚掌握能够多大程度地正确测量我们所需要测量的运动能力，这叫做测量的妥当性。同时，同样的测量者用同样的测量项目，对同一个孩子们进行反复测试所得到的值的一致程度，这叫做信赖性。并且，不同的测量者对同一个孩子施测时获得的值的稳定性与一致性，这叫做客观性。测量实施的简便与容易程度叫做实用性。建议我们要拿出保证如上特性的测验来进行测量。另外，想要得到准确的测量结果，向施测者传达正确的测量方法是很重要的。对于体力、运动能力的测量，在幼儿面前做示范是很重要的。而且，把测量时使用的语言变换成幼儿常接触的易理解语言能够加深他们对测量指示的理解。

（11）孩子们如果受了伤或发生其它事故了，首先沉着冷静的应对是很重要的。幼儿对疼痛或医疗处置十分害怕，也会因此变得焦躁不安。无论是对受伤的孩子还是其它在场的孩子，不要慌乱冷静处理并获得孩子的信任是很重要。

手指戳伤或扭伤，是指因强大的外力或剧烈运动所造成的组织过度被拉伸，造成的骨头和关节周围的肌肉、肌腱等受

到损伤状态。伤后要立即用 RICE 方法来处置。

R（Rest）：冷静下来

I（Ice）：冰敷

C（Compress）：按压固定

E（Elevate）：抬高受伤部位（高于心脏位置）

（12）　如果从开始就给幼儿提供一个给他们感觉到"自己好像做不到"的运动情景，那么就不能调动起孩子的积极性。所以要给孩子们设立阶段性目标，让孩子体验到"自己做到了"这样的成就感，就能够激发孩子运动的热情和丰富孩子的内心体验。在考虑给孩子们设置运动环境的时候，让他们能够开开心心、安安全全地进行运动是最为重要。检查游具或运动器材是否有老化或破损之处的同时，实际地去使用一下以确保安全也是不可或缺的。如果是室内环境，要检查是否有会让孩子磕伤碰伤的棱角之处，或是地板的老化破损之处。如果是在室外，不仅要检查游具还要检查整个活动空间，对于存在危险隐患的地方要进行修理、除去或禁止使用等对策。老师对于幼儿，也要从日常中就教育他们怎样安全地使用游具或运动器材，以及留意运动场所的安全性。

（13）　体育专业领域里的幼小衔接课程，把"让孩子在幼儿期和儿童前期（小学低年级）积累多种多样的运动体验"视为根本。考虑课程的目标时，不是从为了提高某一项运动技能的角度去思考，而是要从让孩子在多种多样的运动中去积累运动体验与运动带来的心理上的愉快体验，从这样的角度出发。总之，要着眼于孩子从幼儿期到儿童期发展的连续性上。

2. 幼儿体育的实践方面

（1） 准备活动英语叫做"warming up"，也就是指使体温升高。通过活动全身、来促进血液循环使能量的供给有效地进行。其结果就会使身体处于体温上升或运动效率良好的状态。当然，对预防受伤以及其它事故的发生也十分有效。先活动离心脏较远的身体部位，进而活动全身。把身体按头、脚、手、躯干这样分开来进行活动，幼儿会很容易理解。同时，也要充分地活动后续将要进行的主运动中所重点使用的身体部位以缓解肌肉紧张。

（2） 做为仅仅使用身体，与同伴共同合作进行、以追逐为基本的四散跑游戏、相互彼此借力得到体力增强的运动、非常受欢迎的儿童瑜伽等动作，对于让幼儿体验多种多样的运动经验、提高调整力非常有效。即使没有道具或运动器材，也能让孩子快快乐乐地体验多种多样的运动。

（3） 像球、呼啦圈、绳子或者是日常生活中的物品（毛巾）、还有一些废旧物品（报纸、购物袋、饮料瓶）等，充分地利用这些开展体育活动，也会让孩子们拥有很好的运动体验。日常生活中的物品与废旧物品也可以摇身一变成为非常好的运动道具，这对于孩子体力的发展以及同伴关系的发展都有很大的贡献。稍微在这方面下一些功夫，孩子的操作类运动技能将会得到很大的发展，这也会使得之后孩子在学习球类运动时所需具备的基本能力得到发展。

（4） 我们把小时候在枯草或莲花草上打滚玩耍、从小石头上跨过、在放倒的圆木或岩石上行走等，通过自然环境而获得的愉快地体验，现在通过移动性游具的使用在户外场地与室内可以再现。在通过垫子、跳箱、平衡木这样移动性游具的使用，让孩子可以体验到现在日常生活中没有机会体验到的旋转感、颠倒感、速度感和平衡的感觉，以一种非常自然的方式来提高孩子操作身体的能力。

（5） 利用固定性游具，通过进行悬垂、在上面上上下下、爬钻等，来锻炼孩子多种多样的运动技能提升基本的体力。对于低年龄幼儿或是智力还未发展完善的孩子来说，只是简简单单地利用这些游具也会让孩子的身体处于运动的状态，对提升孩子的体力是非常有效的。但是有必要去彻彻底底地交给孩子安全的使用方法。

（6） 环境对孩子们的身心发展有巨大的影响，在环境中获得的经验对于孩子以后的生活也会造成很大的影响。我们要给孩子创造这样的环境，即不光要考虑到孩子们身体上的发展，也要考虑社会上、智力上、精神上以及情绪上的多方面的均衡发展。因此，要了解区域活动、组合活动、过障碍物的活动、循环活动等的特征和不同，以迎合孩子生长和发育的水平和需要来区分使用。另外，我们为孩子努力创设这样的运动环境，那就是能够让孩子比例均衡地体验移动类、平衡类、操作类、非移动类活动的环境。

（7） 在运动会中，需要强调孩子们在幼儿园里学习的正确运动应有的样子，和进行正确运动的必要性，为大家创造共同相

幼儿体育需要了解的重点内容　37

互学习的机会。特别是把这些在运动会这样特定的日子里让大家共同进行，让更多的家庭或社区的人知道是非常有意义的。运动会的项目一般分为竞技项目、表演类项目、表现和韵律项目3种。

(8) 对于幼儿期的体育指导来说重要的是，必须优先考虑如"幼儿有什么样的心动体验了？"、"幼儿的心情是什么样的？"，让孩子有心动的体验。也就是说，要把在孩子进入小学前就具备小学体育应有的心理准备状态。也为了避免孩子在入小学后面对那些"因为做不到也不想做"的运动而失去想要尝试的积极性，在入小学前就要让孩子相信自己"只要努力就能做到"，培养孩子的运动效能感和自我肯定感。

关于幼儿体育指导方法的见解

1．活动前的注意事项

（1） 创设安全的环境

确保充足的活动空间，确认过不会和旁边的人或物品碰撞到以后再进行活动。另外，在活动开始之前，要和孩子说明关于安全的一些注意事项。如果孩子的服装不整齐，为了安全起见需要整理服装之后再开始活动。

根据运动的场所是户外或室内、面积的大小，指导内容和方法也必须做出调整。当然进行危机管理也是很必要的，如果是室内要注意玻璃或家具的位置，如果是室外要确认有没有掉落的一些东西，有没有一些坑洞或土块之类的，在指导前要把这些危险隐患都予以除去。另外，在狭窄的室内进行指导的时候，为了防止孩子之间相互冲撞到，将孩子们分成半数予以指导，或选择适合于该场地进行的运动内容，显得非常地有必要。

关于幼儿体育指导方法的见解　39

（2）服　装

运动时服装上需要注意的是，①是否穿着容易活动的服装、②有没有穿得很厚重、③在户外是不是戴着帽子、④鞋子有没有穿好，有没有脚踩鞋跟、⑤要做垫上或器械类运动时，头上是不是带着发卡儿。发现改正这些问题之后才可以开始运动。

指导者也不要忘记自己的穿着。当要求孩子们"请将衬衫塞进裤子"的时候，指导者本身也需以身作则，不要为了时尚而把衬衫露在外面或在地板上脚穿袜子进行指导。如果脚穿袜子进行指导很容易滑倒受伤。加之，指导者还要辅助小朋友，这样的话就更加地危险不可行。也就是说，指导者本身要有成为孩子榜样的意识。另外，为了不划伤小孩子的脸或身体，指导者要把佩戴着的手表或首饰摘下后再进行指导。也要注意挂在脖子上指导用哨的绳子。为了避免绳子缠绕到孩子，不要把哨子挂在脖子上进行指导。对于带帽子的衣服，有可能会妨碍到孩子的视野或动作的进行，所以也要尽量不去使用。为了不划伤小孩的脸和身体修剪指甲也是很重要的。

（3）**指导者的站位**

在户外进行指导的时候，要注意太阳的位置和风向。如果指导者在让孩子听讲解时让他们站在迎着太阳光或风的位置，孩子就会感到晃眼或寒冷，从而影响孩子的注意力。另外，在孩子的视线内，如果有其他正在玩耍的孩子或有车辆的出入，孩子的注意力就会被转移到那里，所以指导者选择的站位，要尽量保证在孩子所朝向的方向不会有影响他们注意力的人和物在内。

特别是在指导小班孩子的时候,指导者在固定的位置进行站位,能够让孩子更清楚明了更加地安心,是比较好的做法。指导者所选择的位置,如果是指导者一发出声音指令小孩子就很容易辨别的位置的话,那么集合和散场就会变得更快更有效率。

(4) 队 形

在指导孩子进行集合的时候,横列队形比较好。因为横列队形能使声音很容易传到后方,并且能让孩子很容易和指导者之间进行眼神交流,增加孩子们的注意力。与此相比,使用纵列队形的话,声音很难传到后方,示范也不容易被看到,孩子也感受不到与指导者的眼神交流。

值得注意的是,无论是哪种队形,有让全体的孩子都进入到指导者的视野当中的意识是非常重要的。孩子脱离指导者的视野,即便是距离再近他们也很难感受到与指导者的眼神交流,注意力难以持续。

(5) 整队与间距

一旦发出集合指令,孩子们都会争先恐后地跑向指导者。大家都想当第一名,都想和喜欢的指导老师挨在一起。这样,如果指导者不预留出背后的空间,在背靠墙的状态下发出集合指令的话,孩子们如果围过来,指导者将动弹不得。让孩子集合的时候,要先站在自己想站的位置稍前点的地方,当孩子们集合过来后,再向后移动几步,与孩子们保持一定的距离。这样,和孩子们保持适当的距离,既能让孩子们看清楚示范动作,也能更好地

进行眼神交流,进而能够更易于进行指导。另外,如果开始和结束的集合位置相同的话,对于小班孩子来说,更容易理解并有利于他们习惯的建立。课程主体进行的场所也固定的话,容易让孩子们很快地静下来。

在整队的时候,孩子们的左右间隔调整好之后,就要调整前后间距。先让孩子们左右伸开手臂保证彼此之间碰不到手之后,接下来主要集中在调整前后距离上,这样能够快速地整好队。

(6) 准备活动

准备活动在英文里是"warming up"。也就是说准备活动是为了让体温上升,通过活动全身来促进肌肉内的血液循环,使能量供给更加顺利地进行。它起到为身体创造一个提高运动效率的状态,也起到防止受伤或出现事故的作用。

在面对孩子示范时,要以相反的方向进行。关于左右方向,指导者需意识到与小朋友的方向相反。另外,像做完顺时针方向跑,接着再做逆时针方向跑时,加入反方向动作能够更好地促进孩子均衡发展,对于丰富和扩展运动内容也很有效。

(7) 分 组

玩雪或滑雪分组的时候,用一般的分组方法即可。但遇到紧急状况的时候,一定要有一个专门守护孩子的人和另外一个负责与外界联络的人,像这样地确保1个组至少有2个指导者。

2．活动展开时的注意事项

（1） 说话方式

指导者充满笑脸创造愉快的气氛，让孩子们感到轻松愉快是很重要的一点。另外，指导者也能和孩子一起从心底享受活动，与孩子在活动的趣味性和愉快气氛上产生共鸣。指导者自身用非常开心明朗的态度进行的话，孩子们的表情也会变得明朗起来。同时为了让孩子偶尔感受到紧张感，指导者变化表情的指导技巧也非常重要。但是，注意不要使用会带给孩子胆怯心理的表情。

（2） 满足感

由简到难需要有阶段性地进行指导。对于小班的孩子来说，只要有小小的进步，孩子们就会有"我学会了"、"我做到了"这样的感受，这是和满足感联系起来的。另外，有必要在不让孩子过多地等待上下功夫。在怎么让孩子排队，怎么摆放用具上下功夫，能减少孩子心理上的一个等待时间。有必要通过使用道具观察孩子怎样进行活动，不拘泥于既成的想法，从某种角度上灵活地进行思考，带给孩子满足感。

（3） 士气的鼓舞

当发现孩子自己努力做出的，对提高体力非常有效等动作的时候，好好地进行表扬能让孩子在教育上获得优越感。我们对于想要努力的孩子做出很好的回应也很重要。对于不能很好地完

成动作或努力想尽办法去完成的孩子也要给予表扬。这样,孩子们就会有勇气去做,被表扬也有利于他们自信心的建立。

在小组游戏当中,一组也不要放太多的孩子。依据孩子年龄的不同各组的人数也会有所不同,4岁以上的孩子,如果是强调相互合作或团队合作的意识每组需要有3-4个孩子,如果是为了理解规则可以进行10个人以内的分组。

(4) 培养主体性、自发性和创造力

给予孩子怎样做才能做得好的建议很重要,但是给孩子时间让他们自己去思考解决对策也很重要。总之,要注意不要过早地教给小孩子答案。为了培养孩子的自主性,不要把答案全部教给他们,要让他们稍微去思考一下以获得答案。另外对于孩子没有做出指导者所期望的动作的时候也不要过于去批评,相反地,要给予表扬并予以承认,这有利于培养孩子的主体性。

同时,要告诉孩子利用身边的一些用品和废旧物品也能有趣地做运动或玩游戏。指导者自身有必要在日常生活中去思考怎样利用身边的物品去做一些道具或用具。

(5) 应对危险

平时我们就要了解用具或器具的安全使用方法以及它的使用方法有多少种。了解关于用具器具的形状或者重量等知识是保证运动安全进行所必须的。当发现孩子们做了不应该做的事的时候,不要以"你为什么要做那样的事呢?"这样责备的方式去对应,应该直接向孩子传达为什么不可以做那样的事。我们要知道

幼儿期孩子头部比例比较大，身体的重心比较高。所以，我们要记住孩子头部比例大容易跌倒这个身体特点，依据此来制作指导计划并进行指导。

（6）竞 争

竞争性的运动并不只是和他人进行比较，而是也要挑战自己。例如，比上次跳得次数多、跑得快、跳得远等等，要重视这些能够激发孩子内在动机的事情。指导者要注重使用能够引起孩子兴趣和易懂的语言，另外说话的时候也要看着孩子的眼睛。1－2岁孩子，因为言语上发展还有限，所以要跟孩子一起动起来，通过做示范来进行指导能够有利于孩子的理解。

（7）对有胆怯心理孩子的关注

对于怀有胆怯心理的孩子要避免强迫他们，另外，对于还做不到的事，孩子努力去做的时候、或是做到了的时候，都要对其努力给予鼓励的话语。

（8）运动量

天气寒冷的时候，为了让身体快些热起来，要选择动作多的项目进行。如果指导者讲话时间过长，会造成孩子身体发冷手脚僵硬的情况，会让他们连技术动作都做不好。

另外，学习的东西过难、通路过窄、没有可以选择的路线、被分配的人数过、可使用的道具少，这些都会使孩子的运动量急剧地减少。在有限的时间内减少等待时间、保证高效地运动，确

保运动量很重要。

（9） 辅　助

当孩子不懂的时候，触碰孩子身体手把手地教，会让孩子更加地容易理解。另外，让孩子感受到辅助和帮助他们的大人身体力量的强大很重要，这能够让他们实际地体验到大人力量的强大和可依靠感，进而让孩子能够更加地感到安心并信赖大人。但是大人要注意力量的增减。

（10） 技术的习得

越是年龄小的孩子，比起语言说明进行实际的示范更容易被理解。指导者让孩子看动作示范的时候，清楚明了地、充分展开地、非常有朝气地去进行非常重要。这样，孩子们看了就会有自己要试试看的兴趣。但是，孩子也会模仿大人不好的地方，所以做示范动作时该伸展的地方要伸展，该弯曲的地方要弯曲。动作简单且能够充分地活动身体为好，可以时而上下活动身体、时而左右转一转、试着改变一下方向。

孩子的积极性和自信是很重要的，大人们要夸大地对他们进行鼓励。对于4岁左右的孩子只给予表扬还不够，对他们清楚地说明什么是好的、什么是不可以的很重要。5岁左右的孩子因为他们自己能够独立地行动了，所以守护住他们变得非常重要。另外需要交给他们一些任务让他们有责任感。

(11) 注意力的持续

幼儿能够集中注意力的时间并不长。1次的指导多在30分~60分之间,同时也会受到年龄、季节和天气的影响。另外,同一种活动项目要考虑控制到10分~15分钟的范围内,不可以长时间进行。因此需要把内容分割在若干个短时间内完成。

关于学习的内容,需要以从简单到复杂的顺序,逐渐递进增加难度。偶尔提高学习内容的难度给孩子造成一定的紧张感,会让孩子能够集中注意力在运动上,也会给他们带来新鲜感。要吸引孩子的注意力,让他们集中精神,指导者声音的大小很重要。不只是用很大的声音去吸引孩子,也有像把声音放低对孩子说"刚才老师说什么了?",这也是一个能够引起孩子的兴趣让他们集中精力的方法。

(12) 创造轻松愉快的气氛

像接力这样的运动游戏活动有一决胜负,活跃气氛的功能。可是,输了的时候要避免孩子们揪住原因不放或是产生攻击行为。在让孩子们做接力运动游戏的时候,考虑到同等地分配人数和男女比例是非常必要的。

3. 整理部分

(1) 整理运动

这一环节主要是为了缓解在活动中被使用的肌肉的紧张状态,调整呼吸及让身心得以放松,减轻疲劳的积聚以保证下次的

活动得以顺利进行。特别是在身体上，要确保通过活动，让处于紧张状态的肌肉恢复它能够顺利进行活动的柔软性，恢复让身体向多种方向弯曲和伸展的柔韧性。不要"因为累了不再去做"，能够好好做整理运动的孩子，能够提高他们变换多种方向做身体动作的能力和柔韧性。应该让孩子形成做整理运动的习惯。

（2） 整理物品

使用很多用具或器材后，让孩子们养成自我整理的习惯很重要。对于孩子来说，那些操作比较难或有一定重量的物品、带有一定危险性的物品、难于收入仓库的物品，应该由指导者进行整理。但是，像球、垫子、轮胎等比较易于安全搬运的东西，孩子们相互合作，可以在指导者的指导下大家一同进行整理。另外，作为指导技巧之一，也有以游戏的形式做整理的方法。

（3） 活动的总结

指导者把教学计划的目的用简单明了的语言传达给孩子，也要对孩子的表现给予反馈和评价。对于孩子们努力了、动脑筋了、积极地活动了这些点，要予以承认进行表扬。相反，对于没有做好的地方，也要给孩子提供一些改善方法，以便于下次活动的进行。

（4） 运动后的安全和卫生保健

要记住在运动过程中跌倒或者是磕破膝盖的孩子，活动完成后要再度确认他们受伤的情况与严重程度，要给出相应的处置

方法。另外,也要让孩子养成洗手、漱口或擦汗等习惯。热的时候要先擦汗后再换衣服。

最后,作为指导者我们要参考这些注意事项来进行指导,和孩子们一起尽情地运动,给孩子们留下美好的运动回忆。

公园运动器材与孩子运动能力的培养

1．夜晚型生活给孩子造成的消极影响

首先，许多孩子被卷入夜晚型生活的现象。在夜晚的大街上，随处可以看到"吃好、喝好、玩好"这样的酒馆看板。我们也常看到父母深夜还带着幼儿出入家庭餐厅、居酒屋（日式小酒馆）以及卡拉 OK 包厢等，甚至还出现设有幼儿玩耍空间及小孩菜谱的居酒屋。试着向家长询问夜里带小孩子出入这些场所的缘由和感受，这些家长的说法是"没关系、孩子还很精神"，"因为晚上是父子接触和沟通的最好时间"，"孩子说不困不想睡"等。所以幼儿很晚还没有入睡的家庭逐渐增加。因此幼儿的生活就陷入"晚睡晚起、筋疲力尽的现象"。在日本，晚上超过 10 点以后才就寝的幼儿比率约超过 40%，这可以说是国家性的危机。

而且，为了成人健身有许多中小学体育馆在夜间开放，大人们带着孩子去那里运动一直到夜里 9、10 点钟，非常地尽兴。孩子们要等着父母运动完后再吃晚饭的例子非常多。被卷入大人们的夜晚型生活而陷入不健康的生活状态，其中一个重要因素是，父母不知道孩子的健康生活节奏本应该是什么样的，非常地

缺乏这方面的知识。

处于夜晚型生活中的孩子，他们的睡眠节奏被打乱、变得没有食欲、也出现了不吃早饭没有排便的现象，这就导致孩子们上午动不起来活动率低下。同时睡眠节奏混乱、不吃早饭、运动不足等情况的出现，会导致自动保护我们的脑或自主神经无法正常地发挥功能与作用，依据自主神经系统进行的体温调节功能也会变弱。所以，如果孩子的睡眠节奏混乱会导致饮食节奏混乱，从而造成不吃早饭和无排便的现象。那么后果就是孩子们会出现从早上开始犯困或倦怠、上午的活动力低下、自主神经系统的调控能力减弱、昼夜体温变化混乱等问题。因此，早上入园时并不能保证体温在36.0℃至36.9℃之间，即出现所谓的"高体温"和"低体温"孩子，早上体温比较低活动率低下，晚上体温高静不下来。

昭和60至62（1985-1987）年，从上午9点到下午4点之间，走路活动的步数约为1万2千步，但是到平成3-5（1991-1993）年时，已经减少到7千至8千步。然而，到了平成10（1998）年以后，大量减少到5千步。现如今，幼儿的步行数已经减少到只占昭和时代（1926年至1989年）的一半左右。而目前因以车代步送幼儿入园的家长人数逐渐增加，在幼儿的生活中整体上步行数减少，必要的运动量不足。

观察幼儿活动时的样子，过圆木或平衡木时，有因脚趾翘起不能保持平衡而掉落下来的孩子。如果在生活中没有充分行走的话，是保持不了平衡的。跑的时候也有同样的现象，出现因膝盖不能抬起而造成足尖拖地的现象，并且也不能很好地挥动手臂。

2. 过多地接触媒体给孩子们造成的消极影响

调查幼儿园小孩子放学后都在什么地方玩耍，第一位的是"在家里"。小学生也是同样的情况，占第一位的也是"在家里"。1年级孩子在家里玩的比例是85%，3年级孩子的比例是75%。就"玩什么"来说，5、6岁的男孩"看电视、录像"占第一位，女孩"绘画"占第一位。进而小学1年级无论男女孩，"看电视、录像"都是第一位，到了3年级以后，男孩"玩电子游戏"，女孩"看电视、录像"占第一位。

看电视、录像与电子游戏，属于在家中进行地不需要活动身体的"对物性的活动"。下午3至5点是体温升高的最佳时机，此时不但没有通过运动让身体得到充分的锻炼，也让孩子失去了学习与人交往这样的"对人性的活动"的机会。也就是说，现在的孩子从幼儿园或学校回到家里也是单独活动很少与人交流。

我们关注孩子们课外活动的方式，看电视和录像、玩智能手机、游戏机等这样的静态游戏的情况越来越多。在孩子们休息的时候，更多地花时间在看电视、看录像和玩电子游戏等等静态娱乐上，导致心、肺、全身的身体机能得不到强化，从而引起体力低下（静态玩耍的时代）。

另外，由于一直凝视屏幕（平面的画面），导致对活动场所的深度知觉和位置关系、距离感的认知能力低下，空间认知能力和自我保护能力就不会得到应有的发展（盯着屏幕的一代），所以与他人碰撞的情况增多。与他人碰撞时也会因日常运动的不足，

做不出收起下颌等这样的保护动作，使得脸部着地而摔倒。另一方面，有些家长即便是说"在让孩子进行运动"，但也只是从小就开始专注于某一项体育运动，而不是让孩子体验多样的运动，所以孩子们是否充分掌握基本的运动技能还存在悬念（运动偏颇的一代）。这样，孩子们过多地接触媒体，会导致他们体力低下、交流能力低下，对还处于成长过程中的孩子造成不利影响。

作为调节孩子生活状况与媒体不良影响的对策，社会上也有提倡创造不触碰电视、录像和电视游戏等的"无电视日"、"挑战无电视日"，通过一定时间断绝同一切电子媒体的接触、进行"走到户外"等活动，来呼吁重视孩子与媒体过多接触所产生的不良影响。可是，只从媒体的利用方式上来下功夫是不能解决根本问题的。也就是说，从幼少年期开始必须让孩子去体会比看电视或玩电子游戏更有趣的、与人有所交流的运动当中。但是，只在形式上给予孩子多种多样的运动体验的指导是不够的。为了让孩子在每节指导课堂里的回忆都有所感动，有必要在指导上反复下功夫和不断努力。我们想要获得孩子们"啊，真有意思，我还想玩！"、"明天，还要给我们玩！"这样反应。这就需要我们提供让孩子们心动的体育活动指导。

另外，不仅仅是指导方法，给孩子提供一个能够安全运动的环境是非常重要的。在闲暇时间，多让孩子们去附近的公园玩耍，通过接触不同的运动器材体验到在公园玩耍的乐趣，这不仅仅对孩子的健康有好处，还可以解决由于夜晚型生活而导致的孩子们运动不足的问题。为了让孩子能够健康地玩耍和体验多种多样的运动，我们要努力让孩子感受到比起"看电视、录像、玩电

子游戏"更有趣的"在公园里玩耍"的乐趣,并带给孩子心动的体验。

3．提高脑和自主神经系统功能的方法

为了让孩子们的脑和自主神经充分地发挥功能,首先要培养大人了解孩子基本生活习惯的意识,和让大人切切实实地能为孩子创造运动的条件。为了提高孩子们脑及自主神经系统的功能,做到以下三点十分重要。

①让孩子们从室内走出到室外,培养他们对周围环境温度的适应能力。

②在像公园等这样的场所,保证运动安全的基础之上,让孩子拼尽全力地去运动,在运动中体验人与人之间的交流。也就是说,在安全的环境中让孩子体验紧急状况下所需的"拼劲全力"地运动的感觉。

③通过运动(活动肌肉)促进血液循环而让身体产生热量(体温上升),通过出汗使身体释放热量(体温下降),不断地给予这样的刺激来激活体温调节功能。

如果要举具体例子的话,如捉妖怪(四散跑)或滚球击人的游戏等是可以让孩子们愉快玩耍的集体活动。还有在公园中利用固定运动器材进行的运动,可以自然而然地对孩子身体施加运动负荷让孩子体力有所增长、运动能力获得发展。这些都能让大脑及自主神经系统的功能很好地调节,让体力自然而然地有所增

长。也就是说，白天让孩子好好地玩耍和运动，能加速胃部排空、调动孩子的食欲并能心情舒畅地很早就想进入梦乡。早睡了第二天就能早起，进而也能早早地吃早饭和入园。有了充足的时间吃早饭，孩子就能获得能量，就会形成使体温升高的良好的身体预热状态，使白天的活动或运动能够顺利地进行，体力也就自然而然地得到提高，这样使身体处于良好的循环状态。

4．公园运动器材的意义和作用

近些年来为了让公园起到促进孩子身体健康的作用，积极地在公园内设置各种能促进健康的运动器材。既可以畅快地玩耍又可以锻炼身体的运动器材，也被作为锻炼身体的运动器材而被利用。这些运动器材无论是广场、公园、街边还是自家的庭院，都可以不需要太大的空间而能简单进行安装。

孩子在心情愉快地玩耍的同时，做多种多样的运动也能改善日常生活中运动不足的情况，也能让孩子体验到运动器材在身边随时就可以玩的便利和乐趣，并且能和家人一起共享乐趣，在玩耍的同时也能获得健康。"公园运动器材"对于提高孩子自主神经系统的功能，培养孩子身心健康发展是十分有效的。在这里，我们思考一下关于它的意义、作用和使用方法，能够培养孩子的哪些能力、以及使用上的注意事项。

公园里设置的运动器材，如固定运动器材是可以通过登、过、滑等，让孩子体验乐趣活动身体的运动器材。通过这些运动器材，可以促进孩子们的身心发展、团队合作能力和例如谦让等社

会的、道德的发展，通过让孩子思考怎么玩运动器材来提高孩子智力上的发展，另外也能培养孩子预测危险的能力和自我保护能力。也就是说，运动器材是能够促进孩子成长与发育的重要设施。当然，对于运动器材来说安全性也是不可或缺的。首先，在安装之前要考虑孩子们的运动轨迹或运动路线，避免孩子们在运动过程中发生碰撞或极度拥挤的现象，保证能够安全并顺畅地使用运动器材。

公园里设置的运动器材及固定运动器材，以促进孩子们的健康、增强体力、陶冶情操为目的，也为孩子提供安全的运动环境。我们经常能见到的运动器材有滑梯、秋千或云梯等等。

（1） 滑 梯

公园或者校园，幼儿园户外场地所设置的标准滑梯，虽然功能简单但是乐趣无穷。从滑梯上滑下来可以提高孩子平衡性与灵巧性等身体调整能力，培养孩子的速度感与空间认知能力。当和小伙伴儿们一起滑下来的时候，还能共享乐趣和增加竞争性，达到互相交流的效果。

（2） 秋 千

秋千是摆动类的运动器材，无论哪个年代都是受孩子们欢迎的一种运动器材。不仅能够让孩子体验到玩耍的乐趣，也能提高孩子的平衡性和掌握多种多样的运动技能。

（3） 云　梯

不仅能锻炼孩子上肢的肌肉力量，也能增强他们全身肌肉力量，培养节奏感及耐力。对于孩子们的身体来说，这是一个身体负荷比较大的运动，那么孩子们就会萌发出一种想去挑战的精神。在云梯下面悬垂移动的时候，对于孩子们身体的节奏感、肌肉和耐力、爆发力的增强是十分有效的。

（4） 造型运动器材和恐龙运动器材

把只能在博物馆中体验到的古代生物或恐龙等搬到孩子的日常生活游戏当中，让孩子能够体验到安全性，也能让孩子体验远远超出化石的真实感。

（5） 模拟爬树的运动器材

再现爬树游戏。作为能够体验爬树的运动器材，充分利用了爬树的有趣之处，特别是设计从一个枝杈到另一个枝杈，或者如果是大型的运动器材，还可以用一些网创造出像迷宫一样的空间。这些会引起孩子的好奇心让他们开始去挑战。模拟爬树的运动器材就是让孩子们不断地经历小的挑战，自己去创造游戏让孩子有更大的梦想。可以让他们体验登、降、悬垂、爬等多种多样的运动。①爬树是集培养孩子"挑战精神"、"运动能力"、"注意力"于一身的运动。孩子们可以爬树枝、进行悬垂等，可以爬往更高的地方体会乐趣，是一种比较安全的运动设施。②可以在两树之间设置一个吊床，当孩子们玩累的时候可以让他们身心得到放松。③当孩子们通过不懈的努力，攀登到树的顶端的时候，可

以感受到舒爽的风迎面扑来,而且通过攀登树木,可以看到与地上不同的风景,可以感受到鸟的鸣叫,这些都会愉悦孩子的身心。

5. 公园运动器材与运动能力的增强

孩子们可以通过公园运动器材达到提升体力、掌握各项运动技能,以及提高运动能力的目的。也可以让孩子们通过自己的想象创造怎么进行玩耍,偶尔也许会有惊心动魄的时候,希望大人们能在旁守候让小孩子尽情玩耍。孩子经过这样的玩耍会很快成长起来。下面介绍一下公园运动器材能够培养孩子的 10 大体力。

(1) 10 大体力

1) **肌力(strength)**

通过肌肉收缩而产生的力,也就是由肌肉最大程度的收缩而产生的力量,通常以 kg 来表示。

2) **爆发力(power)**

爆发力是瞬间产生的能够进行运动的能力。

3) **耐力(endurance)**

耐力包括肌肉在承受负荷的状态下,代表运动能够持续多长时间的肌肉耐力(muscular endurance)、和长时间保证全身运动的呼吸循环系统的耐力(cardiovascular/respiratory endurance)。

4) **协调性（coordination）**

指两个以上的身体部位来协作完成、应对身体内外刺激而进行运动的能力，在学习复杂运动的时候起很大作用。

5) **平衡性（balance）**

是指保持身体姿势的能力，包括在跑、跳等的运动过程中能够保持身体姿势稳定性的动态平衡能力，静止状态下的保持姿势稳定性的静态平衡能力。

6) **敏捷性（agility）**

是指快速地移动身体、转换方向、对刺激所产生反应的能力。

7) **灵巧性（skillfulness）**

灵巧性是指身体所做出的正确的、灵敏的、流畅的运动，就是指灵敏与技巧。

8) **柔韧性（flexibility）**

身体可以向各个方向弯曲和伸展的能力。有好的柔韧性能够使运动顺利且完美地进行。

9) **节奏感（rhythm）**

对音、节拍、动作的反应以及合着声音的高低完成一系列的完美动作，与运动的协调性和效率有关。

10) **速度（speed）**

指物体运行的快慢。

（2） 4种基本的运动技能

对于孩子们来说必要的运动技能分为4种。第一种是像跑、跳等移动类的运动技能。第二种是像过圆木或平衡木等保持平衡

的运动技能。第三种是像投球一样的操纵物体的运动技能。第四种是悬垂于单杠或云梯之下保持身体不动的运动技能。如果孩子特别擅长单杠,但是如果移动类的运动技能不好,那么在活动的过程中,建议可以诱导孩子们进行捉妖怪、赛跑等活动,可以使孩子的运动能力得到均衡的发展。

① 移动类运动技能:走、跑、跳、爬、垫步、游泳等等,从一个地点移动到另一个地点的运动技能。
② 平衡类运动技能:保持平衡、保持姿势稳定的技能。
③ 操作类运动技能:投掷、踢、打和取等作用于物体、操作物体的运动技能。
④ 非移动类运动技能:场所没有发生改变的运动技能,悬垂、原地的推拉等。

(3) 运动时培养的能力

在公园运动器材运动过程中能够被培养的能力。

1) **身体认知能力(body awareness)**

对身体的各部分(手、足、膝盖、手指、头、背部等)与肌肉运动的理解和认识能力。即认识自己身体是怎样运动、处于何种姿势的能力。

2) **空间认知能力(spacial awareness)**

对自己以及自己所处空间的认知,对身体与方向、位置关系(上下、左右、高低)的理解能力。如果能让孩子有效并安全地利用固定运动器材,孩子的体力、运动能力和运动技能将会有适当地提高,不仅如此也能避免受伤或事故的发生。

总之，为了培养孩子健全的身心，①让孩子们拥有良好的运动环境，②要通过运动器材让孩子投入到运动当中，这两点非常的重要。

6．关于公园运动器材基本的安全管理及使用方法

为了保证运动器材的安全性，日常维修是十分重要的。日常维修是指定期地检查设备、以及对产品的构造要熟悉，对于比较难以进行检验的地方要请专业人员来进行检查和修理，这些都是要做到的。另外，即使是安全的道具，不恰当的使用方法也会造成事故。所以我们要在熟悉运动器材安全的使用方法基础之上去指导孩子是十分重要的。当然不仅仅是对于孩子们，对于幼儿园的老师们以及体育指导老师，甚至对与孩子们相关的所有大人，也一定要告诉他们关于游乐设施的安全管理的知识，以及基本的安全使用方法。

首先，为了保证运动器材的安全必须确保活动所需的空间。当孩子从运动器材上滑下来的时候，在落下来的空间范围内除了运动器材本身，不要设有照明灯、井盖、路牙等设施，也不要有诸如石子或玻璃渣等异物。让人兴奋不已的运动器材带给人冒险的情景（可以预测到的危险），可以激发孩子的挑战心理，能够通过多种多样的运动和游戏使得身体运动能力得到进一步的提高。但是也要消除无法预测的"潜在危险"。潜在危险是指和运动器材的挑战因素没有任何关系而存在的危险。潜在危险分为物品危险和人为危险两类。

物品危险是指因运动器材的不恰当的构造与安装，没有很好地去维修管理而产生的问题。人为危险是指在使用运动器材的时候，孩子们相互打闹推搡，或者因诸如手套或鞋子的穿戴而产生的危险。

　　这些危险在孩子们的玩耍当中都是无法预测到的危险，所以运动器材设施的设计者、管理者以及父母，做到防范于未然是十分必要的。要能正确地使用运动器材并能和小伙伴们一起开心玩耍。当运动器材出现异常时，为了保证孩子们能够安心地使用运动器材，除了可以由专门的检查人检查外，也可以让指导老师进行检查。

　　当觉得运动器材出现异常的时候，一定要与管理者联系，家长也应该做到这一点，及早发现及早应对有助于防止事故的发生。从幼儿期开始也要教导小孩子当有螺丝松动或有异常声音发出的时候，要及时地告知附近的大人。另外，对于立体运动器材来说，建议周围也要布置一些网来保护孩子，也有必要考虑使用现在高分子合成塑胶，它可以减少孩子跌倒时产生的伤害。

　　另外，即使是安全的运动器材，使用方法不恰当的话也会引起孩子受伤或其它事故的发生。需要指导老师在了解运动器材的安全使用方法上进行指导。以确保孩子们对于游乐设施的安全使用，并对孩子们进行相应的指导。关于安全的指导方法，不仅仅需要幼儿教师或体育指导老师进行了解，也需要与孩子有关的其他人进行了解。在孩子自由玩耍的时候，大人也要和孩子做好相关的约定。例如，①鞋子要穿好，防止从脚上脱落下来。②要摘下像围巾一样容易被挂扯到的穿戴。③不要敞着外衣的扣子进行玩耍。④放下书包再进行玩耍。⑤不戴有绳子的手套。⑥不要

从上面往下扔东西。⑦不要从高的地方跳下来。⑧不要把绳子绑在运动器材上玩耍。⑨不要在潮湿的运动器材上进行玩耍。⑩不玩破损的运动器材，要把破损之处告诉大人们。

Part II

Daily rhythm improvement strategy: Encouraging the "Eat, be active and sleep well" movement

1. Three problems faced by children in recent years

(1) Sleep rhythm out of order

The first concern is that more and more children in today's Japanese society are becoming night owls. It is now a common sight to see children brought to family restaurants, pubs, karaoke bars, etc. by their parents late at night. Some pubs have even begun to provide designated areas and special menus for children. In fact, growing numbers of parents are letting their children stay up late, saying things like "No problem. Our children are full of life", "Night is the quality time when children can stay with their father" or "Our children say they are not sleepy yet." Consequently, today's children increasingly tend to "go to bed late, wake up late and always feel tired!"

The fact that more than 40% of Japanese young children go to bed after 10p.m. is a national crisis in Japan. The problems here are "lack of knowledge" and "low awareness," causing parents to be ignorant about healthy lifestyles for their children and preventing them from helping their children maintain natural daily rhythms, as well as the nocturnal lifestyles of many adults, which lead their children into unhealthy lifestyles.

So, what actually happens when young children do not sleep long enough less than ten hours at night? These children, particularly short-sleeping ones who sleep less than nine and a half hours, tend to demonstrate behavioral characteristics, such as being less able to exercise caution or concentrate, easily becoming irritated, or being hyperactive and constantly on the move. Such children can neither keep their composure nor properly take part in kindergarten activities, and are likely to have trouble focusing on their lessons after moving on to elementary school.

(2) Eating rhythm out of order

When children go to bed late at night and wake up late in the morning, they are lacking in sleep, they often fail to have a full breakfast or even skip breakfast all-together. This is the second concern.

Skipping breakfast can make children irritable and cause young children to demonstrate behaviors such as throwing building blocks, treating their toys roughly and suddenly hitting friends from behind. Today, however, only 80% of Japanese young children have breakfast every morning. At the same time, increasing numbers of children are failing to have bowel movements at home to make a fresh start in the morning before arriving at kindergarten, resulting in many children not showing up in good spirits. When this is the case, it is no wonder that children are less active in the morning. Reduced physical activity leads to a decline in the daily amount of exercise and prevents children from appropriately building up their physical strength.

(3) Lack of exercise

The third concern is that there has been a marked decrease in the amount of exercise taken by children in their daily lives. For example, the number of steps walked by an average five-year-old nursery school child from 9:00 a.m. to 4:00 p.m., which was about 12,000 in 1985〜1987, dropped to 7,000〜8,000 in 1991〜1993. The number fell below 5,000 after 1998 and the current amount of physical activity done by young children has become less than half compared to the Showa period (1926〜89). In addition, as it has become more common for children to travel to and from nursery school by car, there has been a decline also in the total number of steps walked by children during the whole day. The result is a lack of exercise that is essential for children to build up their physical strength.

2. Body temperature rhythm affected by autonomic nerves and hormones in the brain

Keeping late hours can disturb the sleep rhythms of children, which, in turn, interrupts their eating rhythms, leading to no breakfast and no defecation. This result of this can be reduced physical activity in the morning, affected by morning sleepiness and fatigue. This can cause not only a decrease in their physical strength, but also impaired functioning of the autonomic nerves, which can upset their day-and-night body temperature rhythms (Figure 1).

This is the reason that there are children with "hyperthermia" and "hypothermia," whose core body temperatures are not maintained at a stable 36°C level since they cannot control their body temperatures, as well as nocturnal children whose body temperature rhythms are disturbed so that they are inactive in the morning with a low body temperature and become active at night with a high body temperature.

Generally speaking, human body temperature maintains a certain cycle in daily life in which it becomes lowest at around 3:00 a.m. at night and highest at around 4:00 p.m. in the afternoon, influenced by hormones in the brain (Figure 2). This circadian variability is one of the biological rhythms that human beings have acquired over time. For example, around 4:00 p.m. in the

> Keeping late hours can interrupt the sleep rhythms of chidren.
> ↓
> Disturbed eating rhythms (No breakfast)
> ↓
> Declines in physical activity in the morning and daily amounts of exercise (Lack of exercise and weakened physical strength)
> ↓
> Impaired functioning of the autonomic nerves that automatically protect the human body
> (Upset day-and-night body temperature rhythms, interfering with autonomous, voluntary behaviors)
> ↓
> Interrupted hormone secretion rhythms
> (Difficulty waking up in the morning, inactivity during the day, and inability to get a good night's sleep)
> ↓
> Higher risk of physical and mental instability
> ↓
> Deterioration of academic performance, declining physical strength, truancy, violence

Figure 1　The flow and onset of problems common to Japanese children

afternoon is the time of the day when people become most active.

This is why I call it children's "Golden Time for Play and Learning." I believe it should be the time of the day in which children exercise their curiosity and look for things that catch their interest, for example nature, animals, sports games—I name it—and lose track of time and enjoy play. By experiencing such enthusiasm, attempting new things and repeating a cycle of creating ideas and putting them into practice, over and over again,

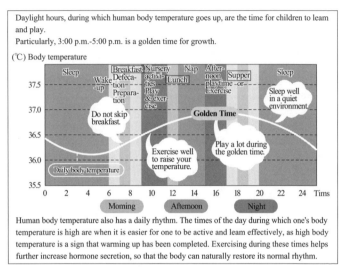

Figure 2 Daily body temperature rhythm

children can achieve dramatic growth.

However, the body temperature rhythms of children who lead nocturnal lifestyles are several hours behind the normal body temperature rhythm. Their bodies are not really awake and are still inactive in the morning, as they have to get up and start the day while their body temperatures are still as low as when they are asleep. The reverse is also true; their body temperatures remain high at night, causing them to have difficulty falling asleep and leading to a vicious cycle.

Restoring these delayed body temperature rhythms back to

normal is the key to the success of the daily rhythm improvement strategy. Here are the two most effective methods of achieving this end: (1) exposing children to sunshine in the morning and (2) getting them to exercise during the day.

3. Launch of the "Go to bed early, get up early and have breakfast" movement and challenges

Put simply, the solution to the problems experienced by children is to get adults to take more seriously the "lifestyles that babies, toddlers and children should have (to achieve a good dietary, exercise and rest balance)." In fact, the "Go to bed early, get up early and have breakfast" movement is a nationwide movement that Japan has developed as the result of its efforts to achieve the above. Although this movement is very effective in encouraging people to take action to promote health, we must admit that it still has room for improvement before it can bring more life to children by proactively stimulating their autonomic nervous systems. Figure 1 illustrates my view of how problems facing Japanese children have developed.

If you want to stop these problems from continuing, the first thing to do is take "sleep" more seriously to help protect and nurture the brains of children. This is why I emphasize the importance of "going to bed early and getting up early." Another important thing is to place special emphasis on "breakfast," as sleep disorders lead to "eating" disorders.

A shortcoming of this national movement, however, is that it only covers these two aspects, while the third one, "exercise," is ignored which is an indispensable part in the daily lives of children if you expect them to be self-motivated, self-directed and able to think and act independently. In fact, exercise and physical play are essential for the development of autonomic functions. It is necessary, also from the perspective of lifestyle improvement, that we should not overlook the importance of providing children with opportunities and occasions, as part of their daily lives, to take exercises during the day to let out their physical energy and release their emotions.

To this end, it is essential that another element, "exercises," should be added to the nationwide "Go to bed early, get up early and have breakfast" movement. To put it plainly, it should be "Eat, be active and sleep well".

In other words, the key is to launch a campaign that emphasizes the importance of "physical activity" and proactively put it into practice. My hope is that children, who are our future, can develop healthy lifestyles and have healthy, fulfilling lives.

4. The importance in meeting new challenges

What is crucial for children now, as a new challenge, is to introduce the importance of "Exercise" into the campaign. The "Eat well, Move well and Sleep well" campaign through the concerted efforts of kindergartens and nurseries with the families and the local authorities, can be implemented nation-wide. It is time that we all join and get involved.

Sports (exercise) and sporting games do not just make one stronger, it improves metabolism, body temperature control and plays an important role in brain or nerve system functions too. It is important that the kindergartens and nurseries, schools and local authorities ensure an environment conducive to sport play where children can play fully engrossed and forget about time – this will help them grow safely. For the sake of a healthy future for our children, it is for society and all adults to work together single-mindedly to provide a good environment for sports and make exercise a part of our daily life. Let's contribute to the hearty effort to make the world a happy place for our children to grow up in.

Why are physical activities during young childhood so important?

1. The problem is not just about physical activities

"The decline in scholastic ability," "the decline in physical strength," and "mental problems." Why did these three issues appear for Japanese children to handle in recent years? When we think it over, we could see the problems stemming from life cycle deficiencies. The society as a whole is becoming a "night person" society, which is making normal sleep cycles impossible. And this leads eating cycles going wrong and so on. When the eating cycles are disrupted and children do not take breakfast, they cannot store enough energy to complete normal activities, and also they lose concentration skills easily. Also, a hungry child loses patience quickly. In these conditions, it is obvious that normal vitality declines. Usually, a body gets tired and then gains strength through activities, which is how humans gain physical strength. Although there are not any chances, and that is why the physical strength declines. Moreover, rest (sleeping), nutrition (eating), physical activities (playing) makes up one day cycle. And when the cycle balance breaks, brain and autonomic nerves, which protects your body, start to work improperly. When this escalates, the hormone balance, which keeps the body temperature, goes wrong. As a result, physical conditioning deteriorates daily, mental function becomes unstable and this leads to "the decline in scholastic ability," "the decline in physical strength," and "school refusal." These culminate in problems of the mind and body.

Today, we've started to figure that these problems about life cycles do not only influence physical strength and physical knowledge, but it also influences mental development. Therefore, when we need to think about "physical activities," we need to look at the whole life cycle, and discuss a better exercise program in detail and the better way of coaching. Young childhood is the time when brain and nervous system develops. So, to firmly establish healthy life habits such as sleeping and eating, and to promote the growth of physical movements and physical knowledge, we must build these habits when the child is young. Keeping this in mind, let's get to work.

2. Impressing experience forms "Liking"

During young childhood, the time when the base of the ability, to form physical knowledge is made, we experience many movements. It is important for the children to feel "I want to do it, I want to play" with a positive will. And by helping to form this positive will, their movements, they wanted to form, becomes diversified, and the movements they worked on by themselves improves during their mid-to-latter period of young childhood. Let's keep introducing many more movements, so that they will keep improving their movements. The experience like "yeah," feeling empowered, when you climb on the vaulting horse, will raise children's confidence to do even more. Please appraise children's movement of feeling of like "yeah," more than what they were able to make or not. Those positive experiences will make them feel that they want to accomplish more new movements. On the other hand, if you kept appraising only the knowledge, and scold just because they could not make it right, this will lead to your child not like exercising. This response can make it difficult to fix the negative experience afterwards.

3. It will even help enough just by watching over

Then, how can we raise children's exercise confidence levels when the children do not have any knowledgeable ability? There is no need to think hard. Just observering your children will help a lot. Children always ask you "Look! Look!" no matter if they are not able to perform the skill. Someone is looking at it. Just watching makes children so happy. Plus, if you cheer them saying "Good job," this will make them feel "I want to try again". And again, they will come over and let you see it, even they are not able to perform the task. In these times, when they are needing contact with people, it will greatly help just by watching.

We have measured how much they are moving by putting a pedometer on the children. During free playing for two hours from 9 o'clock to 11 o'clock, the pedometer measures about three thousands steps. Although, when the play surroundings are set up more interestingly, the pedometer measures up to five thousands steps. And when teachers play together with them, the pedometer measures up to over six thousands step. In other words, when the teachers are with them, and play with them, laugh with them, and promote a positive play experience, the pedometer will probably measure higher exercise and step levels. Even before discussing whether the teachers have the requisite coaching technique or not, it is just a matter of whether teachers are watching the children or not.

With the number of children decreasing, and the society changing, we do not see children playing around the local area as much as before. In spite of that, just by saying "Play freely," physical gain will never expand. So, this is the time when teachers become the leader and play and coach new physical games. This will lead to the children playing more, and will foster much more physical movement. With vitality and physical strength gains, children will naturally become vigorously more active.

Although, if that does not work, it means that the problems are the play settings and surroundings and the teachers willingness to get involved. We need to face it sincerely, and think about what we should do.

4. Society, life cycle, and children's bodies correspondingly coaching to the various changes

When one goes wrong, life cycle also goes wrong. On the other hand, when one goes good, it improves, that is life cycle. When you want to fix the life cycle, exercise and playing are very effective. Problems with today's children are related to a lack of physical stimulus at an appropriate time during the day. At what time period and what kind of physical games should teachers provide? Also, the behavior of the adults who are involved in the physical games and what kind of "words" they use to motivate the children will become very important. We should never forget the point that the physical games will activate life itself. Before, there was a time when it was thought that "health is health," "life is life," and "physical activity is physical activity" all different and separated things, but it is now time to think of it under the relationships. It is becoming important to see how many teachers are seeing the problems and what are they doing to fix the problems. How are the coaches, who are teaching young children's physical education, do they only think about the improvement of physical movements and physical strength, are they employing an already old-fashioned idea? How much do they understand about our changing society, life cycles, and children's bodies, and what can they do to coach corresponding to that change, that change is needed now.

To solve the various children's problems from the root, we should never neglect the life cycle, rest, nutrition, physical activities, and the teachers who could support the development of children are very necessary.

Suggestions for physical education instruction methods for young children

Introduction

Having considered noteworthy points on physical education guidance for young children, I would like to make suggestions to contribute towards the development of early childhood physical education guidelines. These are noteworthy points to keep in mind when guiding and teaching exercises to young children.

Noteworthy points on physical education instructions for young children

1. Noteworthy points at the introductory scene

(1) Safe environmental setting

Ensure safety by securing sufficient space by checking if people or things around the young children may be hit during the exercise. Also, let's discuss ground rules or conventions on safety before starting. If a child's clothing is not in order, only get started after the clothing is properly set.

Teaching contents and methods are to be changed according to whether the location of instruction is indoors or outdoors and whether the area is large or small. Consideration for crisis management is also necessary. If indoors, take note of the position of glass and furniture. If outdoors, be aware of hazards leading to falls, including holes and gaps. Be sure that dust, and the like of it, is not particularly a concern. Remove dangerous items prior to starting.

(2) Clothing

Clothing during exercise should ① allow easy movement, ② be not too thick, ③ include a cap or hat if outdoor, ④ have shoes properly worn and not just be slipping in at the heels, and finally, ⑤ if exercising with exercise mat or equipment, please ensure that long hair is properly secured with hairpin or hair bands on the head.

Please do not forget that the instructor/teacher himself/herself is to pay proper attention to his/her own appearance. If the teacher tells the children to tuck their shirts into their pants, but he himself leaves his shirt untucked due to fashion, this will not be a good example. Guys should be reminded not to wear socks on a slippery floor, and should be careful. If the teacher himself slips and falls, he may be injured. And assistance from the children can be hazardous, and first of all should not be considered. Therefore, it is of foremost importance for the teacher to consciously become a model for the children.

In addition, the teacher should help to remove watches from wrists and accessories from the faces and bodies of the children, and instruct them so. Care should be exercised regarding the whistle hanging round the teacher's neck, ensuring that its string does not end up winding around a child. Hooded clothing hinders vision and movement, and should be avoided. It is also important for the teacher to cut nails so that they do not scratch or hurt a child's face or body.

(3) Teacher's standing position

When teaching outdoors, it is necessary to pay attention to the position of the sun and the direction of the wind. If the teacher's standing position is such that the sunlight or wind directly hits the front of the children listening to the instruction, the child will be dazzled, cold, and lose concentration. Let children try to be positioned with the sun and the wind behind them.

Also, if there are other groups of children who may enjoy playing in front of the children who are in a session, or there may be the coming and going of cars that enter their eyes, the attention of the children are transferred there and the concentration is deprived. Therefore, decide on a standing position so that there are no people or things taking attention away at the front of children.

In particular, when teaching young children, it is good to give a clear standing position, that is, a position where the teacher stands at the time of gathering, to make it easy to understand and secure. When the teacher's voice is issued, it becomes easier for children to predict that the teacher will be in this particular direction, which will make gathering the group easier and make time more efficient.

(4) Formation

When giving guidance and instructions to children, the better formation to gather them in is the horizontal long formation. When the children gather in this landscape orientation, your voice will reach them easily even if the distance is vast, while the children's eye contact with the instructor is easy, enhancing the concentration of the children.

On the other hand, if you gather the children in a long vertical line in front of you, your voice will have difficulty reaching the children at the back in a distance, and movement is also less visible. Also the nuances of the teacher will not be felt by the children. What is critical is to form a formation that allows all members of the children's group to be within the view of the teacher, regardless of formation. If you are out of the field of view, even if the distance is close, it is difficult for the children to see the teacher, and the children cannot concentrate.

(5) Alignment · distance to children

When the children are called to gather, the children will run towards the teacher each one trying to be at the front, with the mindset of "I want to be number one, " or "I want to stick with my favorite teacher". In this situation, if the teacher does not make for enough space behind himself when he calls out to the children, for instance if he stands with his back to the wall, he will have no room to adjust his position in response to the children.

Therefore, when gathering the children, the teacher stands a little in front of his final intended position to accept the children. After a while, he tries to keep a certain distance from the children by taking a few steps behind. In this way, by taking a moderate distance from the children, movement is easy to show, eyes are easy to meet with the children, and it becomes easier to teach with clarity.

It is important for children to form habits with easy-to-understand contents – keep the place to meet at the start as also the same place to meet at the end. By ensuring that the consistent place is used from beginning and end as the spot for explanation, the atmosphere will be kept calm.

When arranging formation, it is a good idea to concentrate on maintaining the distance between the children in front and the back after arranging and taking the appropriate distance interval between the child and the children on the left and right in the row. If you try to line up each child so that neighbors cannot reach one another, next it will be easier to concentrate on just taking the distance in front and behind, and you will be able to line up quickly.

(6) Warm-up

We call the preparatory movement "warming up" in English. In other words, it is to raise the body temperature, move the whole body, improve blood circulation of the muscles, and smoothen energy supply. It is to bring about the state of the body that improves exercise efficiency, so it will be a condition that avoids injury and helps accident prevention. Move the body parts far from the heart, move the whole body gradually, and let's expand the range of motion of the joint.

When doing it face-to-face, it is important to be conscious of opposition always, such as left and right, up and down, in the direction of movement. Also, if you run clockwise, incorporating the movement in the opposite direction, such as running around anti-clockwise this leads to better balanced development. It also works effectively on the accumulation and spreading out of teaching content.

(7) Grouping

The same group should be maintained when going for play with snow and skiing. In an emergency, at least two teachers must be secured for each group with one person looking after the children and the other person turning around for communication.

2. Noteworthy points in the development scene

(1) Manner of speaking

Let the teacher get the interest of the children with easy-to-understand phrases. Look into the children's eyes when talking.

In the case of children aged 1 to 2, it is difficult to communicate in words, so it is a good way to promote understanding by instructing while moving at the same time or showing examples.

(2) Consideration for the fearsome child

Avoid using excessive force on a child who is afraid. Also, even there are things that a child cannot do despite pushing and trying hard, offer abundant praise. Even if all that can be done is just by sitting or watching the guidance nearby, let's try to offer words of encouragement for that effort.

(3) Momentum

When it is cold, let the body warm up by moving the body more. If the teacher's talk is long, the body of the child will be cold, it will lead to injury and cannot offer the opportunity to practice motor activity skills well.

Also, if, for instance, the assignment is difficult, the passageway is narrow, there are no courses to choose, the number of people assigned is too large or the equipment is small, the waiting time becomes long and the exercise amount drastically decreases. In a limited time, it is necessary to reduce latency and make it possible to move efficiently and to secure momentum.

(4) Assistance

Where a child does not understand, if you teach by specifically moving the child's body or touching it, the movement will become easy to understand.

It is also important for children to feel the size and strength of adults who will assist and help them. Children realize the strength and dependability of adults' power, and are more reliable and reliably involved. But please also moderate power.

(5) Mastering skills

It is easiest to show movement with children of lower ages than to explain by words. When the teacher makes a movement to the child, it is important to express it clearly, big and energetic. Then, the feelings of trying will come to the children. However, children also imitate the bad habits of adults. Movement shown as an example must be good and firm movement. In particular, it is important to stretch firmly and bend it enough when bending.

Movement is easy, and things that can move the body to the limits are good. From time to time, let's change the direction by moving the body up and down or turning.

Since motivation and confidence are necessary, I will praise children with exaggeration. When it comes to a 4 year old child, it is important not to praise only but to explain what is good and what is wrong. When children are five years old, they will be able to act for themselves, so they need to be watched over. By leaving enough degree of autonomy, they also acquire a sense of responsibility, so you need to give them good hints on how to act.

(6) Sustained concentration

The time that young children can concentrate is not long. As a guide, a lesson can often be up to one hour long, while the attention span can range from 30 minutes, but such is also influenced by the child's age, weather and season.

Also, let's think of the first event of activities at around 10 to 15 minutes. Since long lasting (attention) is impossible, we are required to promote (attention) while changing contents in a short time. It is sometimes desirable to make the tasks more difficult, make the tasks with moderate tension, to motivate the children to move. It is important in terms of focusing on freshness.

The volume of voice is important to attract children to teachers and to keep them focused. In addition to attracting with a loud voice, there is also a way to make the voices small, dare to say "what did you say?" to make the children interested and concentrate.

(7) The making of a pleasant atmosphere

It is a big point to make children feel "fun" by acting with smiles and creating a fun atmosphere. Also, it is important for teachers to work together to enjoy activities from the bottom of their hearts and feel empathy with the fun and enjoyment of the activities.

When the teachers themselves face each other with a delightful and bright expression, the facial expressions of the children will also become brighter. In order to make children feel tense, it is also necessary to have techniques in which teachers change their facial expressions. However, try not to make facial expressions that would make children afraid.

(8) Feeling of satisfaction

We will move step by step from gentle to difficult things. For young children, if you proceed with a small step, the feeling of "I understood" and "I made it" will lead to satisfaction.

Also, we need ingenuity not to let children wait too much. Let's not let children wait psychologically by ingenuity such as how to arrange children and the position of equipment.

It is necessary to observe how the children are playing with tools, not to be caught in the established concept, but to have flexible thinking from all angles in order to make children feel satisfied.

(9) Stirring up motivation

If you find good movements that lead to children's devised movements and physical fitness, the teacher will highly praise the movement and give educational superiority to the child.

It is important for the teacher to respond fully to the child trying hard. If children are doing well or doing their best and if children are devising, you are to praise that highly. Then, children will motivate themselves and lead to self-confidence by praise.

Depending on age, the number of people in the group to recommend differs, but if children are over 4 years old, a group of 3 to 4 people to cooperate and to make them conscious of the team is good. If you want children to understand rules and regulations of the activities, it would be better to group up to no more than 10 people.

(10) Fostering independence, spontaneity and creativity

It is important to give advice on how to do it well, but it is also important to give time and make the child think about solutions.

The point is that you need to be careful not to teach your answers too quickly. In order to raise an independent child, I would like you to engage in such a way that you do not give too manyanswers and children think about it and can find the answer. Relationships with children who refuse to (blindly) concede to adults and admit it admirably will nurture the independence in children.

In addition, it is important to inform children that it is pleasant exercise and play even if you use an apparatus and recycled (waste) materials. Day by day, the teacher needs to make efforts to devise the kinds of handmade tools and playthings that can be created using something close to us.

(11) Response to danger

Always let the children know about how to use, as well as how to safely use the tools and equipment. It is essential for development of safe exercise to learn the shape, weight of tools, instruments and knowledge about them.

When paying attention to a child who has done a dangerous bad thing, it is not a good way to reprimand with the question of "why do such a thing?", but to tell and stress why such a thing cannot be done or the importance of what should not be done.

In early childhood, it is necessary to understand that the head is large and the center of gravity is high. Therefore, planning and guidance with the features of the child's body in mind are required, with attention that the head is bigger and children easily fall down.

(12) Competition

In competitive exercise, do not just compare with others, but let's make it challenging for oneself. For example, I would like to value my child's intrinsic motivation, such as jumping more times, running faster or jumping farther compared to last time.

Relay style exercise places an emphasis on victory or defeat, and it seems to be exciting at first sight. However, if one loses, avoid pursuing the cause and making it a personal attack. Consideration is necessary to equalize the number of people and the proportion of males and females when playing relay activities.

3. Ending scene

(1) Cooling down exercise

Let the child relax the muscle tension used in the main movement, arrange the breathing of the children, and let the mind and body relax. Try to reduce the accumulation of children's fatigue so that the next activity can proceed smoothly. Especially, in terms of the body, it restores the softness of the muscles which smoothly moves after the former straining. Also, let's ensure the softness of the body by bending and stretching the body in various directions.

Even if children say "do not do it because we are tired, ", you do need a cool down exercise. Cool down exercises make children securely handle the organizing movement and can enhance the physical ability with springs that can create movement from various directions. Let's make it a habit.

(2) Clearing

After using various tools and playthings, I would like the children to have a habit of cleaning up by themselves. For children, the leader should clean up things that are heavy weight, dangerous things and things that are difficult to store in warehouses or equipment boxes, etc. However, for children, items such as balls, cones, mats, tires, etc is manageable. It is possible for children to cooperate with each other and carry them together under the supervision of the leaders who ascertain what they can safely carry.

Also, as one of the teaching techniques, there is also a way to finish the packing and disposal as a last sensation of game.

(3) Summary of the activity

Let the children aim to reflect and evaluate the aims planned by the teacher in easy-to-understand words.

The teacher acknowledges the children's effort, devised ideas and good moves. On the contrary, the teacher will also listen to what children did not do well; let's finish with tips on how to improve.

(4) Security after the exercise and hygiene

During the exercise, the teacher remembers the fallen children, the children who scraped their knees, etc., and after confirming the degree, then check the degree and condition of the injury again. Then, the teacher will take actions and measures such as allowance and necessary observations according to the state of the child.

Also, the teacher instructs children by hand washing, gargling, sweat wiping - let's make these a habit. When it is hot, let the children to remember to wipe sweat thoroughly and change clothes.

Then, while referring to these items of concern, exercise with children and shed a good sweat - enjoy. Teachers and leaders should give their children a lot of fond memories to bring home.

Park play equipment and raising children

Introduction

The current trend in park play equipment in recent years has been to actively introduce healthy playthings as a means to improve the health of public park participants. Park play equipment that can easily move the body while remaining fun can also be used as a training tool for health promotion. While using the feeling of playful free play, you can move the body vigorously, it helps to eliminate daily exercise shortage and promotes physical fitness. If healthy park equipment is available, you can enjoy the ease and pleasure of using it. Plus, families can enjoy it and they can become healthy while playing too.

In this article, I will focus on park equipment and children's health, and I would like to promote my idea to support the growth of children. Specifically, we introduce health management problems that children in recent years have experience and analyze the significance and role of "park play equipment" and its effectiveness for improving problems, what is the best method of utilization and the best way to improve park playground equipment and notes on use.

1. Health management problems held by children in recent years

(1) Negative influence on children by pursuing an adult nightlife

In recent years, children are caught-up in the night life of adults. When you come out to the city at night, you will see a sign for a bar, "Eat, Drink, Enjoy (Relax)!", "Completion of Private Room with Kids Space". It looks fun, but children are being taken by their parents to those place I often see small children entering or leaving at midnight from family restaurants, taverns, convenience stores, karaoke boxes, etc. I've heard: "It's okay, because the child is fine.", "Because the children are having fun.", "Because night is the time of contact between the father and the child.", "Because the child says he is not sleepy yet". The number of families who are letting their children stay up late is increasing. Currently, a child's life is "late to bed, getting up late, and going to bed stuffed!"

Also, parents have their young children in school gymnasiums that are open for adult health recreation, many adults start enjoying exercise in these exchanges from 9 o'clock to 10 o'clock in the evening. Many children in these situations do not have dinner until after their father or mother finish their sports. In these situations, children are getting into the night life of adults and are becoming unhealthy. Parents are ignorant to facts about healthy children's life rhythms. Parents need to know that they should not try to have their children match their adult life rhythms. I want to "sound the alarm" to parents with a lack of knowledge on this recent trend.

Children, in many cases do not have dinner until their parents are finished playing their sports. There are situations where children are getting into the night life of adults and are becoming unhealthy, parents do not know how a child's healthy life rhythms should be, they need to know that they cannot match their children's rhythm. The facts need to be brought to the attention of parents with small children. In the evening, when children disrupt sleep rhythms their food does not advance, and it causes scarcity and defecation. As a result, the activity strength in the morning declines and it becomes impossible to move.

And with sleep disorder, absence of taste, lack of exercise, the function of the brain and autonomic nervous system which automatically protects the body does not work well, the temperature control which is controlled by the autonomic nervous system cannot successfully function. After all, the body temperature does not fit in the 36 degrees range, so-called body temperature cannot be adjusted "children with high body temperature" and "hypothermic" children, body temperature rhythm shifted, body temperature cannot move in the morning, body temperature rises and starts to move children and more movement will come to be seen.

Among them, what is worrisome is that the children's momentum is drastically decreasing. For example, although it is the number of steps of a 5-year-old child in a nursery school, in the Showa 60 to 62 period, around 12 thousand steps have been moving between 9 a.m. and 4 p.m., but since Heisei 10, it entered 5 thousand steps, and it drastically declined to about half the exercise amount in the Showa era.

Besides, the use of cars in downtown gardens has become more frequent, so the number of steps in the whole life of the child is decreasing, and the required exercise amount is greatly reduced. When looking at the activities of children, children who are falling cannot keep the balance of their feet, as the toes of the feet float when walking on a log or walking the average table top. These occurrences are unthinkable if they walk enough in their lives. Even if they run, they cannot raise their knees securely, so they rub their feet on the ground and hook it. Moreover, their hands are always stopping, not helping in their movement.

(2) Negative impact of excessive media contact on children

Looking at the playgrounds for young children after kindergarten, the first place is inside the house, 85% of the first graders and 75% of the third graders are in the house, even primary school students are staying indoors. The majority of the play for toddler boys is TV/video, for toddler girls drawing is No.1. When you advance to the first grade, both boys and girls are TV/video. And for third graders, the boys are playing video games and the girls using TV/video.

TV/video viewing and video games are objective activities that do not move the body while in the house. 3 to 5 o'clock in the afternoon after school, although the body temperature is rising at a great pace, not only are the children not fully using the body, but also opportunities for learning from interpersonal relationships are lost. In other words, even after returning from the garden or school, the children now work individually and do not have enough interaction with people.

When static play is employed by children; TV, video, smartphone, and game equipment increases during leisure time, the heart, lungs and whole body are not strengthened, causing physical strength reduction (static playing generation). Also, because they stare at the screen (flat screen) and one point, the ability to recognize the depth, positional relationship and sense of distance of the activity environment is immature, spatial cognitive ability and safety ability do not develop as required (screen generation). So, there are many important reasons to get children in contact with "actual" people.

Even if they say "I am exercising", since they are specialized in a single sports from a young age they do not experience diverse movements, children who do not have basic motor skills in a well-balanced state, (There is also concern about the existence of biased generations). In this way, excessive media contact also threatens the growth of children in the process of development, such as lower physical strength and lower communication ability.

Under such circumstances, as a response to children being barraged by the media environment in society, parents should start employing a "No TV Day" or "No TV Challenge" to make a day for not touching television, video, video games, etc. For a certain period, all electronic activities such as "out media" that breaks contact with images and challenges something else, a call is made to break off excessive media contact by children. However, simply focusing on devising methods of media usage will not fundamentally solve the problem. In other words, from the early childhood years, children must enjoy the pleasures of exercises involving people, not to be overrun by the draw of television, video, games and so on. However, it cannot be done without parental guidance that needs to include a variety of exercise experiences to get children in shape. We need to devote ourselves to efforts and guidance so that positive memories of one frame of guidance will be an exciting experience that remains in the minds of children. From children, "Oh, it was fun, I want to do more" "I want to do it again tomorrow", parents must provide guidance that will render positive impressed reactions so that the children will want to come back. I am painfully promoting the necessity of teaching parents to actively employ the minds of children through movement.

In addition to teaching methods, making safe environments where exercise can be accomplished is extremely important for supporting children. Going to a familiar park in leisure time, playing with playground equipment in the park, and experiencing the fun of playing in the park not only contribute positively to a child's health and memories, but also helps with night rhythms. It greatly contributes to solving sleep-type problems associated with exercise shortages. For the purpose of experiencing healthy play and exercise, I would like to emphasize the essentiality of "park play" and its positive experience to a child's fitness experience.

2. How to increase the work of children's brain and autonomic nerves

In order to ensure that the brains and autonomic nerves of children work properly, first of all, it is necessary to create awareness for the adults who monitor the basic lifestyle habits of their children. They are in charge of scheduling exercise environments in which children can actually move their bodies. It is necessary for adults to seriously work on making time for daily exercise for their children. In order to enhance the function of children's brains and autonomic nervous system, I recommend three practices.

① Make children adaptable and responsive to various environmental temperatures by outdoor activities, not inside the home.

② To have a solid experience of "exercise involving people" that moves and responds actively in a safe playing place like a park.

③ Through exercise (muscle activity), blood circulation improves, generates heat (raises body temperature), dissipates perspiration, releases heat (decreases body temperature) and stimulates to activate the body temperature regulating functions.

If you provide concrete examples of exercise, you can enjoy

"fun and active" collective play such as tag and rolling dodgeball, these activities put loads on the body naturally through the play games mentioned above. Using physical strength, movement skill and activities using "fixed playground play in the park" will be extremely effective. These activities will improve the function of the cerebrum and autonomic nervous system and lead to the enhancement of physical strength naturally.

In other words, during the day, when the sun is out, children should play by moving the body and exercising. This will promote hunger in the child, then after a quick dinner, the child will be tired and go to bed early. A non-adult sleep rhythm will allow the child to get up early, eat a good breakfast and start their day energized and earlier. Because there is time to eat a scheduled breakfast, energy is gained and the body temperature is raised further, daytime activities and exercise can be started, physical strength also promotes good circulation which increases naturally.

3. Significance and role of park play equipment

Exercise equipment installed in the park, among them fixed playground equipment, it should include apparatus that includes climbing, crosses, ladders, and slides so the children can enjoy the benefits of actively moving the body. Children, through playing with this equipment will nurture their mental and physical development, social and moral skills, such as the development of cooperation skills. Cooperation and concession with friends, intellectual development to devise ways of playing, together with the danger prediction ability and safety will allow each child to develop these abilities.

In other words, the park playground is an important life-stage that promotes the growth and development of children. Overall, the park playground is a playground equipment (facility) made for the purpose of promoting children's health, physical strength, enriching emotions, to provide children with safe and sound playing scenes and exercise scenes. Everyone, as you know, there are slide tables, swings, bows and so on, as well-known playgrounds and facilities.

(1) Slide stand

The slide, which is standard equipment in most parks, school gardens, and garden courts has a simple function, but it is fun for all. By sliding down the slide, children will enhance the body's ability to adjust, it improves equilibrium and dexterity, and will cultivate the sense of speed and the cognitive ability of space. By sliding down with friends, they can enjoy themselves and compete with others while interacting with other children.

(2) Swing

The playground swing is familiar to children of many generations. It is not only fun, but also improves the body's ability to improve the weakening balance kids are experiencing in recent years.

(3) Monkey bars

Not only improves upper body strength, but it also will strengthen the overall muscular strength and nurture the sense of rhythm and endurance. It is a playground apparatus that creates exercise that puts a relatively strong load to the body of children, but it is a plaything that works on challenging the spirit of children's "challenge". By hanging on the bars and traveling, they will increase muscular strength, rhythmic feeling, endurance and instantaneous power, as well as rhythmic feeling to make movement more efficient.

(4) Monument playground equipment · dinosaur play equipment

Ancient creatures and dinosaurs that can only be seen in a museum are coming to children's playground. Children can experience exercise safely while playing in the presence of real fossils.

(5) Tree climbing playground equipment

Dynamic tree climbing can be reproduced. As a plaything, your child can experience the climbing of a tree, the fun of climbing up the tree, especially branch-to-branch. For safety, a net is tensioned spirally and it also creates a playing space like a maze. Of course, children inflate their curiosity, climb up branches and start climbing toward the sky. Tree climbing play equipment repeats small challenges as many times as possible, creates play and fosters children's dreams. Children can experience diverse movements such as climbing, descending, hanging and crawling.

① Tree climbing is an athletic playground item that children in their growth years can acquire a "challenge spirit" "exercise ability" and "concentration ability" all at the same time. It is a playground apparatus that they can feel the fun of climbing to high places and the realistic challenge of tree climbing safely while climbing branches and hanging. ② When they are tired of playing, falling down, the net will change quickly to a hammock and wrap their body gently. ③ Climb the tree and reach the summit, they can feel the refreshing wind. Also, as an observation facility imitating a natural tree, it is a noticeable landscape different from the ground, and it is also a point of wonderful bird watching that they can hear birds' singing as well.

4. Ability to be cultivated with park playground equipment

Children, by playing with playthings, will increase physical fitness, gain various motor skills and will greatly improve motor abilities. Also, from the imagination of children, we may develop different types of play, and sometimes it may be a little frustrating, but I would like you to play a lot while watching. That experience will make children grow more and more. We introduce 10 physical fitness factors, four basic exercise skills, ability to grow up during exercise by children playing with park playground equipment and exercising.

(1) 10 physical fitness factors
1) **Strength**……I express it in kg whether a thing of the power to occur by a line shrinking that is a line can show how big power by the greatest effort.
2) **Power**……used in the word power, refers to the ability to generate a momentary exercise by instantaneously exerting force.
3) **Endurance**……the muscular endurance of how long the work can be continued under the load applied to the muscle group, and long-term exercise of the whole body. The

cardiovascular / respiratory endurance of the respiratory and circulatory function that is continuously performed can be broadly divided.

4) **Coordination**······refers to the ability to combine the motion of two or more parts of the body into one cohesive movement or exercise in response to stimulation from the inside or outside of the body. This plays an important role in learning complex exercises.

5) **Balance**······use of the word balance refers to the ability to maintain the body's posture. In the movement of walking, jumping and crossing, it is distinguished between dynamic equilibrium which means the stability of posture and static equilibrium which means stability of the body in a stationary state.

6) **Agility**······It is the ability to quickly move the body, change directions, or respond to stimuli.

7) **Skillfulness**······It is the ability to move the body exactly, quickly and smoothly according to the purpose, so-called dexterity skillfulness.

8) **Flexibility**······It is the ability to bend and extend the body in various directions by the softness of the body. With superior flexibility, you can do exercise smoothly and beautifully.

9) **Rhythm**······It is a condition including sound, beat, mo-

vement, or unreasonable beautiful continuous motion, related to coordination and efficiency of exercise.

10) **Speed**······It is the speed at which an object moves.

(2) 4 basic movement skills

In order to foster athletic ability, I would like to have 4 exercise skills as a necessary action. The first is a type of exercise that runs, jumps and moves. The second is an exercise that balances, like a log crawl or walking an average railroad rail crossing. Third, an exercise to manipulate things like catching a ball. The fourth one is exercise where you do not move the body while hanging (static) from the iron bar or monkey bars. It is necessary for the growth of a child's body that all 4 types of exercise are incorporated daily. Movement stimulus that is conscious of the play environment are moving, equilibrium, manipulating, and not moving. If you are good at a (static) steel bar, but you are not good at moving, you should invite that child to "play tags and bonds" in fun play. It will promote the child's ability to acquire well-balanced movement skills, increase their exercise capacity at the same time.

1) **Locomotor movement skill**: It is a technique to move from one place to another, such as walking, running, crawling, jumping, skipping, swimming and so on.

2) **Balance skill**: It is a skill that keeps posture stable, such as

balancing, rail crossing, etc.

3) **Manipulative movement skill**: It is a technique of movement that acts and manipulates things, such as throwing, kicking, striking and taking.
4) **Non-locomotor movement skill** (sports skill on the spot): It is a technique of hanging, pushing and pulling on the spot.

(3) Ability to grow during exercise

Parents should aim for their child to grow physically during regular exercise with the help of proper park playground equipment.

1) **Body awareness**······It is the ability to understand and recognize the body part (hands, feet, knees, fingers, head, back, etc,) and its movement (muscle movement). It is the ability to figure out how your body moves and how it relates to your posture.
2) **Spatial awareness**······It is the ability to understand your body and the space surrounding it, understand the direction and position relation (up and down, left and right, high and low, etc.) with your body. Children's physical strength, athletic ability, and physical exercise skill will properly increase if children make effective use of fixed playground equipment safely. In addition to that, it also naturally leads to the prevention of injuries and accidents.

   In essence, in order to raise children of sound mind and

body, it is important to (1) correctly arrange the children's exercise environment (playthings) and (2) practice appropriate exercises to train the body using these playthings.

(4) Safety management (basic) of park playground equipment and safe usage

Even if it is a safe plaything, if children use it improperly, injury or accident will occur. It is required to know the safe usage of playground equipment and to teach them to use the equipment properly. Of course, not only for children, but also for teachers at school and teachers of physical education guidance. In essence, all adults involved with children, to include fitness leaders, should be very familiar with each piece of sports playground equipment. They should all have knowledge of basic safety management and the useful techniques and skills associated with all playground equipment safety procedures.

For the safety of the playground equipment, first of all, prior to installation, carefully arrange the movement flow of children. The flow line and the play equipment, should flow so that when children hit the merges so their movement does not become extremely clogged with children. It is important that consideration is given to the arrangement and placement so that children can develop fun play safely and smoothly with playground equipment placement.

It is also extremely important to secure the space required for activities (securing safety areas). Note the height that is supposed to be reached when a child falls or jumps off of playground equipment. In this space, except for the playground equipment body, there must be no facilities such as lighting lamps, manholes, curbs, or any foreign objects such as stone and glass.

Risks of exciting playthings (predictable danger) will arouse children's desire for meeting the challenge, and under these circumstances, they will further enhance their physical abilities by doing various play and exercises. However, it is necessary to eliminate unexpected danger "hazards". A hazard is the danger that occurs in places that are not related to the challenging elements of playground equipment. There are two types of hazards: physical hazards and human hazards.

The physical hazard is the danger that there is a problem with inappropriate placement and structure of playground equipment, poor play equipment due to insufficient maintenance and management. Human hazard is when there is a problem with the method of using the plaything, such as playfully pressing when playing equipment is pushed together, wearing gloves and shoes with cords that can get tangled easily. These dangers are unpredictable dangers in children's play, and adults such as designers, administrators and playground monitors need to be aware of them beforehand for preventive purposes.

Also, use the playground equipment properly, let's play together. When there is a problem with the playground equipment, in order to be able to use the playground equipment with peace of mind, in addition to inspection by a specialized company, we would like the playground monitor to do frequent inspections. If you are using playthings and feel there is the potential for a problem or incident, it is important to contact the administrator. Early detection and early response will lead to accident prevention, so cooperation from adults is necessary. When screws are loose or abnormal noise occurs, it is important that children are instructed from early childhood to instantly inform adults in the vicinity. In addition, we recommend that you enclose solid playground equipment with a net.

In addition, it is also necessary to plan to reduce the burden due to injury when falling by using urethane material. Even if it is a safe plaything, if children use it incorrectly, they can get injured. It is required to know the safe usage of playground equipment and to teach the children. It is an obligation that all people using playground equipment that all people involved with children should know. It is necessary to be strict on this requirement.

For example, ① Always take off hard-soled shoes, ② Take off things that easily get caught like mufflers, long shoestrings, scarfs etc., ③ Do not leave the front of the coat open, ④ Do not take school backpacks on the playground, ⑤ No string or rope,

⑥ Do not throw objects from above, ⑦ Do not jump off the heights, ⑧ Do not wind string around playground equipment, ⑨ Do not play on wet playground equipment, ⑩ Do not play with broken playground equipment, and tell an adult about defective equipment.

Finally, in order to use playground equipment safely, daily maintenance is important. Implementation of daily maintenance, periodic inspection is paramount for a safe playing environment. Furthermore, it is important to ask the expert or playground administrator to repair or improve the structural integrity of the playground equipment in order to make it safe for everyone.

Children's health and welfare strategy in Japan

We have been accumulating children's mental and physical problems from questionnaire surveys taken from all around Japan. And now, we are working with the local administration (e.g. Board of Education, childcare section, and lifelong study section etc.) and organizations related to childcare and education, to plan a practicable project and put it into practice.

For this national project, 2011 is the year when the life rhythm improvement strategy "Eat, be active, and sleep well!" should be spread and implemented all around Japan.

POINT1: Propagation of the theory of recent children's problem appearance

【THEORY 1】

When children's sleeping rhythm goes wrong, it becomes harder for them to eat breakfast, then eating rhythms also start to collapse. Additionally, the function of autonomous nervous system will become weaker, and it would be hard to protect the body automatically.

Soon, the rhythm of hormone secretion would start to collapse. In this condition, children can not act voluntarily and independently. The physical condition would work badly, and the mental health would be easier to become unbalanced. The decreasing of scholastic ability and decrease of physical strength would lead to rise in mental problems recently seen in children.

Life rhythm improving strategy, "Eat, be active, and sleep well" as a slogan.

【THEORY 2】

Life is connected by a cycle, so when one starts to go wrong, others start to collapse. But likewise, when one thing in life improves, soon others start to improve also. Therefore, in the time when the sun is up, in the daytime, children should move their body and play actively, and do physical movements. Soon this increased activity would lead to hunger. Children would desire to have their dinner soon, and become tired comfortably, which leads to early bedtime. Moreover, when children go to sleep earlier, it would be possible to wake early the next morning. Consequently, the eating of breakfast and the school attending time would also become earlier. Since there is enough time to eat a full breakfast, children would be able to gain energy and would be able to start their day with enough "warm up" energy by warming up their body temperature and finally, this would promote good circulation.

When fixing the life rhythm, the sunlight in the morning and physical activity in the afternoon is one of the effective sources. Do not give up and pick one goal for improving the problem. Let's start working out for improvements toward each problem one by one. All of the child's rhythms would absolutely improve. Let's work hard with our slogan "One point breaks through, everything improves."

POINT 2: Proposal of 3033 practice

We would like to share a proposal of "3033 practice." 30 minutes a day, 3 times a week, and 3 months of continuous exercise, this will lead the autonomous nervous system to start working correctly.

It is even fine to add the physical activity of 10 minutes and totaling 30 minutes. The way to feel the expectation of physical effect, it is better to not cram physical activity in the beginning of the week such as Monday, Tuesday, Wednesday. What is important is that you continue the physical activity habit constantly.

POINT 3: Spreading of family exercise

The practice of "Family exercise." First, make a time for families to play and exercise with their children. Let children have the time to monopolize their parents. Let them sweat with their parents. Praise the things children are working hard on and let the children feel confident. Also let the children think and create the movement by themselves. Family exercise will also rectify the problem of bad eating and sleeping rhythms.

Family exercise is a practice that has taken place in many areas. But to work out seriously, the district, society, community, prefecture and country, need to seriously start working together for the big movement of children's health construction.

Part III

演讲

婴幼儿健康生活的重要性
—饮食、运动以及充足睡眠—

前桥 明

早稻田大学
教授/医学博士

日本幼儿体育学会
会长

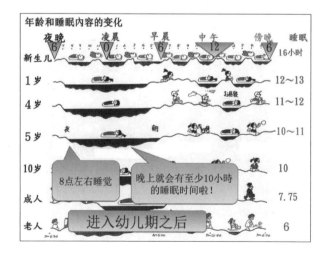

婴幼儿健康生活的重要性 — 饮食、运动以及充足睡眠 — 125

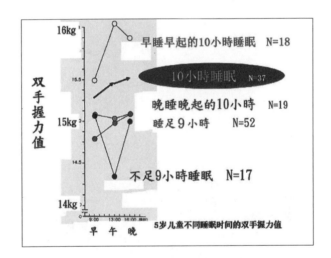

5岁儿童不同睡眠时间的双手握力值

低于9小时30分的短时间睡眠儿童（幼儿）的特征

注意力不能集中
烦躁不安
不能安静地待在一个地方
走来走去

（前桥・石井・中永，1996＿）

婴幼儿健康生活的重要性 － 饮食、运动以及充足睡眠 － 127

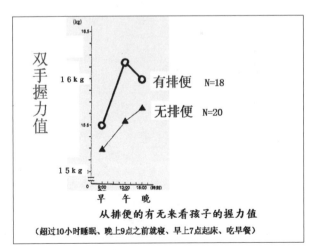

从排便的有无来看孩子的握力值
（超过10小时睡眠、晚上9点之前就寝、早上7点起床、吃早餐）

婴幼儿健康生活的重要性－饮食、运动以及充足睡眠－

电视・影像、电视游戏的普及
（盯着屏幕的一代）
空间认知能力・自我保护能力得不到培养

智能手机、移动手机
（玩静态游戏的一代）
体力得不到提升

拘泥于某一项体育活动
（运动内容偏颇的一代）
缺乏丰富多样的运动体验
4种运动技能掌握不全

如此，体力得不到提升，空间认知能力得不到发展。受伤之类的事情屡屡发生！

Q：为什么早上没有精神反而晚上精神而不睡的孩子越来越多了呢？

因为到了晚上体温还很高！了解了关于体温的变化后我们就懂了！

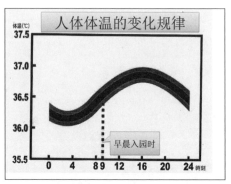

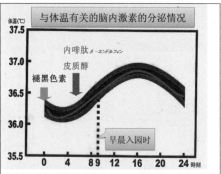

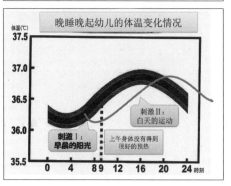

婴幼儿健康生活的重要性 － 饮食、运动以及充足睡眠 － *131*

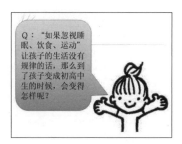

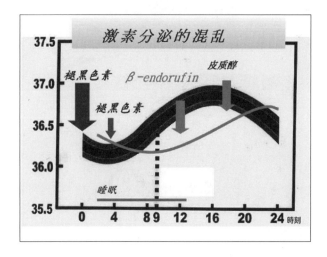

激素分泌的混乱

早晨起不来、白天不想动。

晚上就睡不熟。

这样的生活将持续下去…

如果睡眠节奏混乱的话

○就餐的节奏混乱（早上不吃饭）
○整个上午的活动力低下
　（运动不足・体力低下）
○自主神经系统功能低下
　（昼夜的体温变化混乱）
○荷尔蒙分泌混乱
○身体不适
○情绪不稳
○学力低下・体力低下・不上学・暴力行为

调整孩子生活节奏的措施
"早睡、早起、吃早饭"运动

Q：号召"早睡、早起、吃早饭、运动"好吗？

如果睡眠节奏混乱的话	睡眠作息规律混乱的情况
○就餐的节奏混乱（早上不吃饭） ○整个上午的活动力低下 　（运动不足·体力低下） ○自主神经系统功能低下 　（昼夜的体温变化混乱） ○荷尔蒙分泌混乱 ○身体不适 ○情绪不稳 ○学力低下·体力低下·不上学·暴力行为	○就餐的节奏混乱（早上不吃饭） ○整个上午的活动力低下 　（运动不足·体力低下） ○自主神经系统机能低下 　（昼夜的体温变化混乱） ○荷尔蒙分泌混乱 ○身体不适 ○情绪不稳 ○学力低下·体力低下·不上学·暴力行为

那么，怎样提高自主神经系统的功能？

婴幼儿健康生活的重要性 － 饮食、运动以及充足睡眠 － 133

内心的寄托

安全·安心感

增强体力

模仿能力

关于亲子体操的小海报

婴幼儿健康生活的重要性 — 饮食、运动以及充足睡眠 —

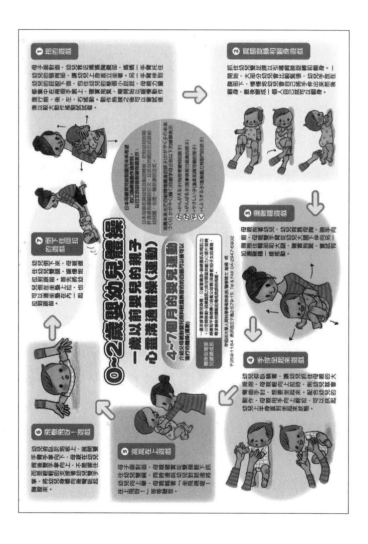

婴幼儿健康生活的重要性 － 饮食、运动以及充足睡眠 －

婴幼儿健康生活的重要性 — 饮食、运动以及充足睡眠 —

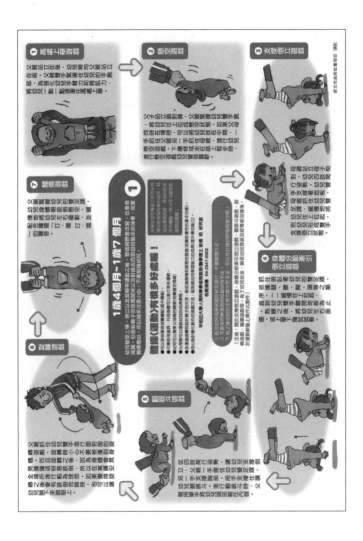

婴幼儿健康生活的重要性 — 饮食、运动以及充足睡眠 —

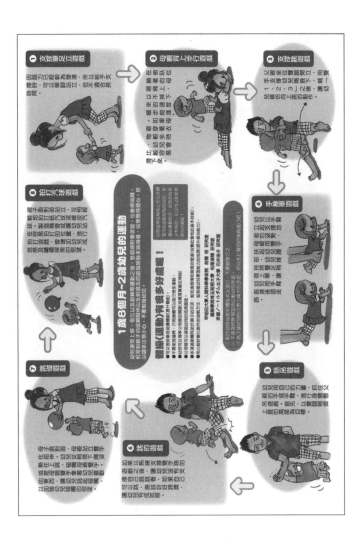

婴幼儿健康生活的重要性－饮食、运动以及充足睡眠－

婴幼儿健康生活的重要性 － 饮食、运动以及充足睡眠 －

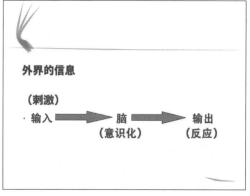

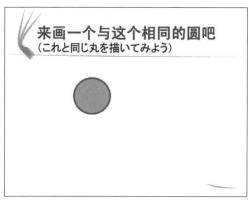

游戏运动与促进幼儿身心发展 — 婴幼儿体力提升 — 149

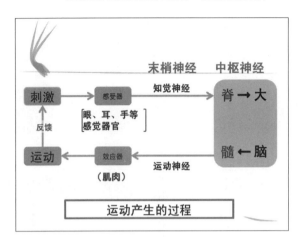

- 感觉的重要性(感覚の大切さ)
- 感觉训练的内容(感覚訓練の内容)

- 认识身体各部分(手、脚、膝盖、手指)和理解其活动（肌肉运动）的能力。
  身体部分(手・足・ひざ・指など)とその動き(筋肉運動的な動き)を理解・認識する力。
- 清楚自己的身体是如何运动的、处于什么样的姿势。
  自分の体が、どのように動き、どのような姿勢になっているかを見極める。

空间认知能力
空間認知能力

- 认识自己身体所处的空间，并理解身体和方向、位置关系（上下、左右、前后、高低）的能力。

  自分の体と自己を取り巻く空間について知り、體と方向、位置関係(上下・左右・前後・高低など)を理解する能力。

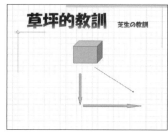

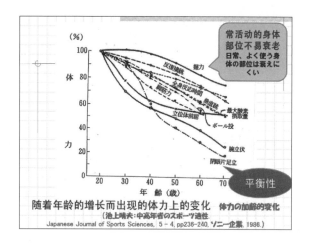

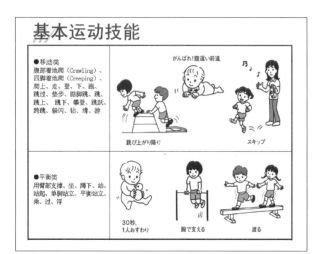

Locomotor skill
移动类运动技能

爬、走、跑、跳、游

Balance skills
平衡类运动技能

Keep the balance,
stand on a balance beam
and get on and pass
保持平衡，
站立、骑坐、走平衡木

站在大腿上保持平衡
もものりバランス

Keep the balance on
mother's knee
站在妈妈的膝盖上部保持平衡

154 Part III

Manipulative skills
操作类的运动技能

Catch, throw, kick, hit and carry

接、投、踢、击、搬

Hit the ball
击球

Non-locomotor skills
非移动类运动技能

(Exercise skill at the place)
Hang/push / pull it on the spot
悬垂、推、拉

吊环云梯

Pull the leg
拉脚

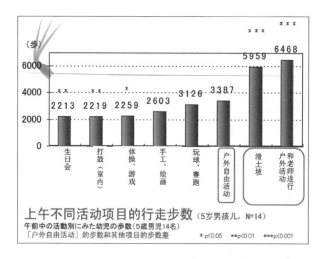

上午不同活动项目的行走步数（5岁男孩儿，N=14）
午前中の活動別にみた幼児の歩数（5歳男児14名）
「户外自由活动」の歩数和其他项目的步数差　　＊p<0.05　　＊＊p<0.01　　＊＊＊p<0.001

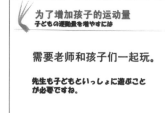

日本幼儿体育学会
幼儿体育指导员资格培训会

幼儿体育是什么

从运动产生的生理机制来看

早稻田大学 教授 医学博士
前桥 明

The International Society of
physical education of young children

以儿童为对象,通过各种游戏或活动、指导活动来培养身心全面发展的社会人。
- 身体的(physical)
- 社会的(social)
- 智力的(intellectual)　mental
- 精神的(spiritual)
- 情绪的(emotional)

所谓的幼儿体育
幼児体育とは

通过各种身体运动（运动游戏、游戏、舞蹈等）从教育的角度对孩子实施指导，以培养身体上的（physical）、社会性上的（social）、智力上的（intellectual）、精神上的（spiritual）、情绪上的（emotional）等多方面均衡发展的、身心健全的幼儿。即社会人的形成。

各種の身体運動(運動あそび、ゲーム、スポーツごっこ、ダンス等)を通して、教育的角度から指導を行い、身体的（physical）、社会的（social）、知的（intellectual）、精神的（spiritual）、情緒的（emotional）な面をバランスよく伸ばし、心身ともに健全な幼児に育てていこうとする営み（教育：人間形成）である。

幼儿期应该体验的运动内容
幼児期に経験させたい運動内容

- 走是"运动之根本",跑是"运动的主角",所以建议给让孩子有更多的体验关于走和跑的运动机会。
- 在日常生活中,孩子们很少有倒置、翻滚、旋转、爬行,支撑等的运动经验,所以要从幼儿期开始,多培养孩子倒置、翻转和支撑这样的感觉。

- 歩くことは「運動の基本」、走ることは「運動の主役」である点をおさえ、もっと歩く・走る経験をしっかりもたせたい。
- 生活の中で、逆さになる、転がる、まわる、追う、支えるといった動きが少なくなってきているので、幼児期から努めて、逆さ感覚や回転、支持感覚を育てていきたい。

角色扮演游戏与体育运动
ごっこあそびとスポーツ

「幼児と運動・あそび」の理解
理解"幼儿与运动、游戏"

★3岁孩子与捉妖怪游戏(3歳子どもと鬼ごっこ)

男孩、女孩的不同情况

★扮演性和游戏性

过家家　　(ままごとごっこ)

幼儿期应该注重适合于幼儿的、角色扮演的游戏、同时加入一些关于遵守社会规则和礼貌的培养。

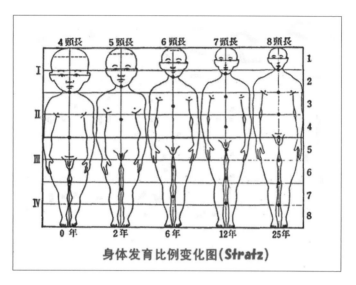

身体发育比例变化图(Stratz)

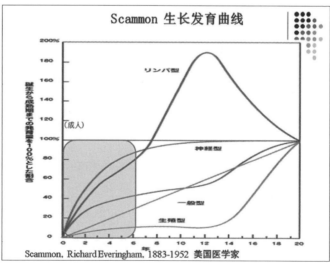

Scammon, Richard Everingham, 1883-1952 美国医学家

幼儿体育指导上的注意事项

日本早稻田大学 教授·医学博士
日本幼儿体育学会 会长

前桥 明

我们整理了幼儿体育指导时的注意事项。

運動を幼児に指導するにあたって、指導上、大切な留意事項を整理しておきます。

关于运动服装的确认：

　　　　運動を行う時の服装として、

①是否穿着有便于运动的服装？ **①動きやすい服装であるか**
②是否穿得过于厚重？ **②厚着をしていないか**
③在户外时是否戴着帽子？ **③屋外では、帽子をかぶっているか**
④是否穿好鞋子、有没有踩着鞋子的后跟？
　　④靴をきちんと履いているか、靴の後ろを踏んでいないか
⑤做垫上运动以及器械运动时，头上是否带发卡儿之类的？
在运动之前能够注意到这些问题并及时纠正是十分重要的。
　　**⑤マットや器械系の運動時に、頭部にヘアーピンをつけていないか
　　　等をチェックして、問題があれば、それらの問題点を正してから始める
ことが大切です。**

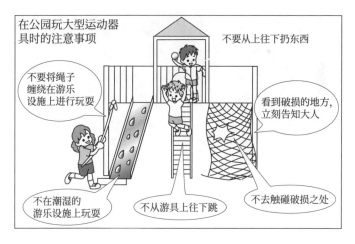

横列队形的特征 　横長の隊形の特徴

将孩子们集中起来进行指导时,使用横列队形比较好。声音容易传到后面,便于更好地与指导者进行眼神交流,也能提高小孩们的注意力。　另一方面,使用纵列队形的话,站在后面的孩子不仅很难听到声音,也看不清指导者做的示范。同时,也很难和指导者有眼神上的交流。

需要注意的是,不管选择怎样的队形,保证所有的孩子都在指导者的视野范围内是十分重要。否则,即使孩子们与指导者的距离再近,孩子感受不到与指导者的眼神交流的话,注意力便不能持续很久。

子どもたちを集めての指導では、横長の隊形で集合させることが良いでしょう。横長に集めれば、後方にまで声が届きやすく、指導者とのアイコンタクトもしやすくなり、子どもたちの集中力が増していきます。一方、縦長に子どもたちを集めると、後方に位置する子どもたちには声が届きにくく、示範も見えにくくなります。また、指導者の視線も感じられなくなります

気をつけることは、どのような隊形でも、指導者の視野の中に、全員の子どもが入るような広がり方を意識することが大切です。指導者の視野から外れると、子どもたちは指導者との距離が近くても、指導者の視線を感じづらく、集中力を持続できません。

当把孩子集中到一起的时候，因为身后没有留出足够的空间，使得指导老师很难做动作。

子どもを集めるときに、背後のスペースを十分にとっていないために、指導者が動けなくなっている

整队・与孩子们的距离　整列・子どもたちとの距離

一旦发出集合指令，孩子们都会争先恐后地跑向指导老师。孩子们都想当第一名、都想和喜欢的老师挨在一起。

这样，如果指导老师不预留出背后的空间、在背靠墙的状态下发出集合指令的话，孩子如果围过来，老师将动弹不得。

让孩子集合的时候，要先站在自己想站的位置稍前点的地方，当孩子们集合过来后，再向后移动几步，与孩子们保持一定的距离。

这样，和孩子们能够保持适当的距离，能让孩子们看清楚示范动作，也能更好地进行眼神交流，进而能够更易于进行指导。

子どもたちに「集まれ」と呼びかけると、子どもたちは我さきに指導者に向かって走ってきます。「一番になりたい」「大好きな先生にくっつきたい」というのが、子どもたちの気持ちでしょう。

そのような場面で、指導者が後方にスペースをとらず、壁に背をつけた状態で集合を呼びかけてしまった場合、身動きが取れなくなります。

子どもたちを集めるときは、自分の立ちたい位置より少し前で、子どもたちを呼んで受け入れ、その後に、自分が数歩、後ろにさがって、子どもたちと一定の距離を保つように心がけましょう。

このように、子どもたちとの距離を適切にとることで、示範も見せやすく、子どもたちとの視線も合わせやすく、さらに、ゆとりをもって指導しやすくなります。

幼儿体育指导上的注意事项　167

不能很好地完成示范。背后没有充分的预留空间

在整理队形时，先确保左右有适当的间隔，再去调整前后距离比较好。

先让孩子们以相互之间碰不到手为准，保持左右间隔进行排队；然后就更容易去集中于调整前后距离，以达到迅速整队的效果。

我们把调整"左右"称做为"间隔"，把"前后"称做为"距离"。

整列するときは、となりの子どもとの間隔を適切にとった後、前後の距離を保つことに集中させると良いでしょう。

隣同士がお互いに手が届かないように、間隔を開けて並ぶようにさせると、次は、前後の距離をとることだけに集中しやすくなり、早く整列できるようになります。

隣とは「間隔」、前後は「距離」と言います。

安全的环境　安全な環境

　我们要确保有足够的空间,不会碰到周围的人或物品,保证自己有充分的指导空间,来进行指导。

　十分な空間を確保し、まわりの人や物に当たらないか、自分も指導のできるゆとりのスペースがあるかどうかを確認して安全に始めましょう。

在室外时,注意是否有掉落的东西,坑洞,砂石等,指导前对于安全隐患要予以排除。

屋外であれば落ちているものや穴があいていたりしないか、砂埃はまっていないか等は、とくに意識して、指導前にとり除ける危険なものについては、拾ったり、動かしたりしておきましょう。

幼儿体育指导上的注意事项　169

请看下这张图片，能看出什么问题吗？
次の指導の様子を見てください。問題点は？

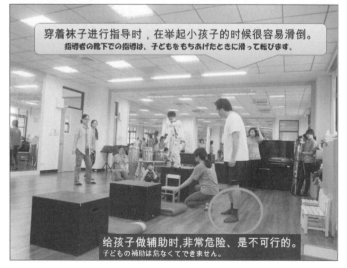

幼儿体育指导上的注意事项　171

要把衬衫塞进裤子里。
シャツはズボンの中に入れましょう。

运动时，会被看到肚子，后背和内衣哟！请整理好服装之后再进行指导。
運動していると、おなかや背中、下着が見えますよ。
服装を整えてから、運動しましょう。

服　装

指导者自身，也请不要忘记自己服装的整齐。指导者在对孩子们说"请把衬衫塞进裤子里面"的同时，指导者自己却为了时尚，把衬衫一直散落在裤子外面，是不可取的。同时，也不要穿着袜子在地板上进行指导。滑倒的话会受很严重的伤。而且，给孩子们做辅助的时候，也是很危险的，是不可以的。总之，时刻要有为孩子们做榜样的意识非常的重要。

　指導者自身が、自分の身だしなみに注意することも忘れないようにしてください。子どもたちに、「シャツをズボンにしまいなさい」と言いながら、指導者自らがファッションにこだわり、シャツを出しっぱなしにすることのないように、また、床面で靴下履きのままで指導しないように、気をつけましょう。滑って転んで、大ケガをします。まして、子どもの補助は危なくてできません。
　まずは、子どもたちの模範となろうとする意識をもつことが大切です。

◆为了不让自己的手表和项链等饰品刮到小朋友的脸或身体，要事先摘掉这些后再进行指导。
◆要注意带绳子的哨子的使用。为了避免绳子缠绕到孩子，应尽量避免把哨子挂在脖子上进行实操的指导。
◆带帽子的衣服，有可能会妨碍视线和动作，也要尽量不去使用。
◆为了避免划伤孩子的脸或身体，修剪指甲也是很重要的。

子どもたちの顔や体に、自分の腕時計やアクセサリーをひっかけないように、はずして指導しましょう。
首からかけている笛のヒモにも、要注意です。ヒモが子どもに巻きついたりしないように、笛を首からぶら下げての実技指導も控えましょう。
フードつきのウェアーでの指導も、視界を妨げたり、動きを止めたりする可能性があるため、控えましょう。
子どもたちの顔や体をひっかいて傷つけたりしないよう、爪を切りそろえておくことも重要です。

在掌握用具或器材的安全使用方法的同时，平时也应该事先了解多种使用方法。
关于用具或器材的形状及重量的知识也应该事先学习，这是保证安全运动所必须的。

用具や器具の安全な使用方法とともに、どれくらいの使用方法があるかを、日頃から知っておきましょう。
用具や器具は、どんな形状や重量なのか、それらについての知識を習得しておくことが、安全な運動の展開には必須です。

幼儿体育指导上的注意事项　173

虽然指导者下了很大功夫来组合这些道具，给孩子创造了新的运动环境，但是，如果孩子们因此摔倒而受了伤害的话，也就谈不上好的环境了。
指導者が工夫して遊具を組み合わせて、新たな運動環境をつくっても、もし、子どもが転んだときに大けがをするようでは、良い環境とは言えません。

脚被绊住，支架倒下来的话是很危险的。
足を引っかけて、支柱が倒れた場合、危険です。

> 指导者要注重使用能够引起孩子兴趣并通俗易懂的教学语言。另外，说话时要看着孩子的眼睛。
>
> 指導者は、子どもの興味を引く話し方やわかりやすい言葉遣いを大切にしましょう。
> また、話すときは、子どもの目を見て話すようにしましょう。

说话时，要看着孩子的眼睛。
話すときは、子どもの目を見て話すようにしましょう。

指导者在给孩子做示范动作的时候，运用易懂的、夸张的、充满朝气的表现方法是非常重要的。

这样，孩子们就有想要自己做着试试看的兴趣。

指導者が子どもに動きを見せるときには、わかりやすく、大きく、元気に表現することが大切です。
そうすると、子どもの方に、やってみようという気持ちがでてくるはずです。

指导者在给孩子做示范动作的时候，运用易懂的、夸张的、充满朝气的表现方法是非常重要的。

特别是，动作上该伸展的地方要充分伸展，该弯曲的地方要充分弯曲。

这样，孩子们就有想要自己做着试试看的兴趣。

但是，孩子也会模仿大人不好的习惯。做示范的时候，认真地正确地做动作很重要。

子どもに動きを見せるときには、大きく、元気に表現することが大切です。
とくに、しっかり伸ばすところは伸ばし、曲げるところは十分に曲げることが大切です。そうすると、子どもの方に、がんばってみようという気持ちがでてくるはずです。
しかし、子どもは、大人の悪い癖も真似をします。見本に示す動きは、しっかりした正しい動きが良いでしょう。

幼儿体育指导上的注意事项 177

简单而又能让身体得到充分活动的动作比较好。来试着改变运动方向，时而上下活动身体，时而扭转一下身体。
動きは、簡単で、しかも、しっかり体を動かせるものが良いですが、時々、体を上下させたり、まわしたりして、方向も変えてみましょう。

营造欢乐的氛围 楽しい雰囲気づくり

给孩子营造一个充满欢笑的愉快气氛,让孩子感受到"欢乐"和"爽朗"是很重要的。同时,指导者跟孩子一同用心去感受,跟孩子在活动的趣味与开心之处产生共鸣很重要。

笑顔で活動して楽しい雰囲気を作り、子どもたちに「楽しさ」や「明るさ」を感じさせることが、大きなポイントです。また、指導者もいっしょになって、心から楽しんで活動することと、活動のおもしろさや楽しさを共感することが大切です。

指导者跟孩子一同用心去感受,跟孩子对活动的趣味与开心之处产生共鸣是很重要的。

给孩子营造一个充满欢笑的愉快气氛,让孩子感受到"快乐",这是很重要的。

指導者もいっしょになって、心から楽しんで活動することと、活動のおもしろさや楽しさを共感することが大切です。

笑顔で活動して楽しい雰囲気を作り、子どもに「楽しさ」を感じさせることが、大きなポイントです。

幼儿体育指导上的注意事项

如果指导者能用开心且充满阳光的表情来进行指导的话，孩子们表情也会变得明朗起来。
指導者自身が楽しそうで明るい表情で向き合うと、子どもたちの表情も明るくなっていきます。

在孩子们有疑问的时候，手把手教的话，孩子会更容易理解。
子どもがわからないところは、具体的に子どものからだを動かしたり、触ったりして教えると、動きが理解しやすいでしょう。

辅助

在孩子们有疑问的时候，手把手地教，孩子会更容易理解。

对于非常努力的孩子，随时关注是非常重要的。做的好的时候，认真努力的时候，下功夫想要做好的时候，都要认真给予表扬。

这样的话，孩子们会充满干劲，也会因为被夸奖而变得自信。

子どもがわからないところは、具体的に子どもの身体を動かしたり、触ったりして教えると、動きが理解しやすいでしょう。
一生懸命しようとしている子どもに、しっかりと対応することが大切です。上手にできている場合やがんばっている場合、工夫している場合は、しっかり褒めていきます。そうすると、子どももやる気をもったり、愛められたことで自信につながったりします。

指导老师的站位

在室外进行指导的时候,要注意太阳的位置以及风向是十分重要的。

相对于还需要听老师讲解的孩子们来说,如果指导老师让孩子站立在迎太阳和风的一侧,孩子们会感觉晃眼或者冷风,使得他们不能集中注意力。

让孩子们处于背对太阳和风向的位置,是我们指导者需要时刻留意的。

指導者の立ち位置
屋外で指導をする場合には、太陽の位置や風向きに注意することが必要です。
話を聞く子どもたちに、太陽光や冷たい風が、直接、正面からあたるような指導者の立ち位置は、子どもがまぶしかったり、寒かったりして、集中力をそぐことになります。
子どもたちが、太陽や風を背にして、位置できるように心がけましょう。

这样的占位比较好!
この立ち位置がいいですね。

- 用具・器具需保持卫生、整洁，保证安全和正确地使用。
- 准备和收拾垫子的时候不要进行拖拽。
- 在残障儿童使用垫子的时候，有必要事前的进行消毒以及清扫。
- 请注意也不要用脚移动垫子。
- 用具・器具は、保健衛生上、きれいに、かつ、衛生的に長く保持できるように、丁寧に扱うとともに、安全保持上、正しく使いましょう。
- マットを引きずっての準備や片づけはしないように気をつけましょう。障がい児に対して、マットを使用する場合は、事前の消毒や清掃の必要な時が多々ありますので、気をつけてください。
- マットを足で動かすこともしないように気をつけて下さい。

幼儿体育指导上的注意事项 183

大家一起齐心协力,抬起并搬运垫子。
協力してマットを持ち上げて、マットを運びましょう。

指导者在进行讲解或做示范动作的时候,可以让大家坐下来听。
話をしたり、見本を見せたりするときは、いったん座らせてから、行いましょう。

沉着冷静、对现场做出很好的判断是非常重要的。
落ち着いて、その場の状況判断が大切です。

让孩子们感受到大人身体的高大和力量的强大是很重要的。孩子切实地感受到大人力量的强大，可以使孩子更加信赖大人。不过，要注意控制力量。

简单而又能让身体得到充分活动的动作比较好。来试着改变运动方向，时而上下活动身体，时而扭转一下身体。

大人の身体の大きさや力強さを、子どもに感じさせることも大切です。子どもは、大人の力の強さや頼もしさを実感し、一層信頼して関わってきます。でも、力の加減もしてくださいね。

動きは、簡単で、しかも、しっかり身体を動かせるものが良いですが、身体を上下させたり、まわしたりして、方向も変えてみましょう。

幼儿体育指导上的注意事项

运动量　　運動量

　　天气寒冷的时候，为了让身体暖和起来，多做一些活动量大的身体活动吧。指导者讲话时间过长的话，孩子们会感到寒冷和冻僵，就会让孩子陷入一个连动作的都做不好的状态。

　　同时，课题过难、道路过狭窄、可供选择的内容过少、每组分配的人数过多、可使用的道具过少、等待时间过长都会导致孩子们的运动量减少。在规定时间内减少等待时间，确保有效率地进行运动以保证运动量是十分关键的。

寒いときは、からだが温まるように動きの多いものにしましょう。指導者の話が長い場合、子どものからだは冷えて、かじかんで、技術すら練習できない状態になります。
　また、課題が難しかったり、通路が狭かったり、選択するコースがなかったり、割り当てられた人の人数が多すぎたり、用具が少なかったりすると、待ち時間が長くなり、運動量が激減します。限られた時間の中で、待ち時間を少なくし、効率的に動けるように配慮して、運動量を確保する工夫が必要です。

幼儿体育指导上的注意事项　187

虽然说，学习内容一般是由简单到复杂，通过慢慢地增加难度来设置的。但有些时候，选择一个难的学习内容，以适当地带给孩子们紧张感，对于能更好地让孩子集中注意力，保持好奇心是非常重要的。

課題は、単純なものから複雑なものへ、少しずつ難易度を増すように配慮してもらいたいですが、時に、課題を難しくして、適度な緊張感をもたせることは、動きに対して集中させたり、新鮮さをもたせる点で重要です。

注意力的持续　集中力の持続

　　幼儿不能长时间的集中注意力。1次的指导时间，从30分钟开始，最长不应该超过60分钟。孩子的注意力也会受到年龄、天气、季节的影响。

　　另外，每一种活动的时间控制在10～15分钟左右比较好。因为时间过长的话孩子很难集中注意力，所以我们建议短时间地适当地进行内容交替的指导。

　幼児が集中できる時間は、長くありません。1回の指導では、30分から長くても60分くらいを目安とすることが多いですが、子どもの年齢や天候、季節の影響も受けます。　また、1種目の活動は、10分～15分くらいの目安で考えていきましょう。長続きは無理なので、短時間で内容を切りかえながら進めていくことが求められます。

> 让小朋友们知道，即使是身边的道具、废旧物品，也能对他们开心地运动与玩耍起到帮助是很重要的。
>
> 身近にある道具や廃材を利用しても、楽しい運動やあそびに役立つことを、子どもたちに知らせることも大切です。

利用纸箱玩耍

幼儿体育指导上的注意事项　189

> 指导者自身在日常生活中也应该努力思考如何利用手边的物品，来亲手制作用具或道具，这也非常的重要。
>
> 指導者自身が、日頃から、身近にあるものを用いて、どのような手づくりの用具や遊具が創作できるかを考案する努力が必要です。

T ball

利用路障
工事用のコーンの利用

即使做不到,在孩子努力认真做的时候,要给予鼓励的话语。
できないことでも、がんばって取り組んでいるときは、その努力に対する励ましの言葉をしっかりかけてあげましょう。

对于胆小孩子的一个特别的关照
恐がる子に対する配慮

- 即使做不到,在孩子努力认真做的时候,要给予鼓励的话语。
- 对于胆小的孩子,避免让他勉强地去做某事。另外,即使是做不到但努力在做,或做到了的时候,要在言语上对孩子的努力给予鼓励。

- できないことでも、がんばって取り組んでいるときは、励ましの言葉をしっかりかけてあげましょう。
- 恐がる子どもに対しては、無理にさせるようなことは避け、また、できないにことでも、がんばって取り組んでいるときは、座るだけでも、見るだけでも、できた場合には、その努力に対する励ましの言葉をしっかりかけてあげましょう。

幼儿体育指导上的注意事项

- 必须营造安全的运动环境。
- 认真做好运动器具的老化排查工作。

安全な環境づくりが、必須です。
遊具の劣化点検を、しっかり行い、子どもの指導に臨んでください。

判断标准　固定用的地基露出来是不行的

判断基準　基礎の露出はだめ

改善吧！
努力吧

运动器具的安全检查(老化问题)
遊具安全点検（劣化）

支柱部分的腐朽
支柱地際部の腐食

木桩部分的腐朽
木柱地際部の腐朽

熔接部分的腐朽
溶接部の腐食

连接部分的腐朽
接合部の腐食

驱动的磨耗、破损
駆動部の摩耗・破損

绳索的破旧断裂
ロープ等の破断

1. 孩子成长的目标与评价
子どもの成長の目標と評価

Q：一个既是孩子成长目标，又能作为评价指标的诊断是什么呢？

孩子成长与发展的诊断

现在孩子们的生活状况是健康的吗？另外，是否有充足的运动，我们要把握这些。针对这样的提问，利用这个雷达图，对于现在孩子生活当中好的部分和有待于改善的部分会一目了然。另外，定期进行测量，可以很容易捕捉到其变化。幼儿园和家庭同时配合记录的话，能够有更精确的诊断结果，对于向父母传达生活和运动的重要性时，也可以使用。

現在の子どもの生活状況が健康的であるか、また、運動あそびが足りているかを把握してみましょう。問いに答えて、このチャートに書き込むと、今の生活でよい部分、これからチャレンジしたい部分が一目でわかります。また、定期的にチェックすることで、その変化も捉えやすくなります。園と家庭が協力して記録することで、より精度の高い診断結果となりますので、生活と運動あそびの大切さを保護者に伝えるきっかけとしても、ぜひ活用してみてください。

「吃、动、充足睡眠!」运动的目的－孩子成长发育的诊断与评价－ 195

诊断方法

1：8-13页的①-⑥按照"是"或"否"进行回答。在幼儿园的时间也要通过同孩子的对话进行记录。

2：回答"是"的一项记1分（满分5分），把合计分数填到对应的项目中。

3：把①-⑥项目的分数填到相应的地方连接成点。

4：连接成的六角形面积越大，代表孩子们的身体状况和生活环境、运动环境、发展状况越好。另外，越接近正六角形，表示各个项目发展的均衡性比较好；六角形越不正的话，各个项目擅长与不擅长，好与不好就越容易看出。

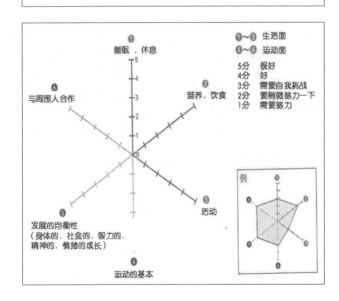

2．诊断的内容
①睡眠・休息

生活篇

① 睡眠与休息

「作为生活基本活动的睡眠、不只是睡眠时间的长短，入睡时间和起床时间都很重要。早上起来的时候，如果能不留前一天所剩下的疲惫，能够清清爽爽地起床很重要。」

睡眠（休息）

- 1. 晚上尽量在9点之前睡吗？
- 2. 每天晚上睡10小时以上吗？
- 3. 早上在7点之前起床吗？
- 4. 早上起床的时候能沐浴到阳光吗？
- 5. 早上起来的时候很精神吗？

回答"是"计1分，5分为满分。共 □ 分

- 1. 夜9時までには、寝るようにしていますか？
- 2. 毎日10時間以上、寝ていますか？
- 3. 朝は、7時までには起きていますか？
- 4. 朝、起きたときに、太陽の光をあびていますか？
- 5. 朝起きたときの調子は、元気ですか？

②营养·饮食

生活篇

② 营养与饮食

「饮食对于孩子成长健康及结实的身体而言不可或缺，只要和家人或朋友们围坐在一起心灵上就能够得到营养供给。每天都为了能吃好做着努力呢吗？」

饮食（营养）

- 6. 每天吃早饭吗？
- 7. 早上都有排便吗？
- 8. 能开开心心地吃饭吗？
- 9. 吃完零食到晚饭之间有2个小时左右的间隔吗？
- 10. 尽量不让孩子吃夜宵吗？

回答"是"计1分，5分为满分。 共 ☐ 分

- 6. 朝ごはんは、毎日、食べていますか？
- 7. 朝、うんちをしていますか？
- 8. ごはんを、楽しく食べていますか？
- 9. おやつを食べてから夕ごはんまでの間は、2時間ほど、あいてますか？
- 10. 夜食は、食べないようにしていますか？

③活动

生活篇

③ 活动

「作为睡眠或饮食以外的日常生活活动,例如像帮忙做一些事或是看电视这样的看似小的事情,长时间的形成并固定下来成为习惯,其影响是不容忽视的。」

活动

- ▶11. 徒步去幼儿园吗?
- ▶12. 在户外,能玩得出汗吗?
- ▶13. 能够为身体运动努力做些什么吗?
- ▶14. 看电视玩游戏的时间,合起来在1个小时之内吗?
- ▶15. 晚上,能够悠闲地泡澡吗?

回答"是"计1分,5分为满分。 共 ☐ 分

- ▶11. 歩いて通園していますか?
- ▶12. 外に出て、汗をかいて遊んでいますか?
- ▶13. からだを動かすお手伝いができていますか?
- ▶14. テレビを見たり、ゲームをしたりする時間は、あわせて1時間までにしていますか?
- ▶15. 夜は、お風呂に入って、ゆったりできていますか?

④ 运动之根本

> 运动篇
>
> ### ④ 运动之根本
>
> 「把握孩子户外活动的量与运动能力。如果不太清楚的话，可以和孩子一起去公园好好地确认一下。」

运动之根本

- 16. 上午有在室外玩耍吗？
- 17. 15～17点间是否在户外玩耍？
- 18. 比例均衡地在做跑、跳、投球等运动吗？
- 19. 能够在单杠和云梯等下面做悬垂，在平衡木上能保持平衡之类的吗？
- 20. 能够享受到玩幼儿园户外运动器械或公园内运动器械的乐趣吗？

回答"是"计1分，5分为满分。 共 ☐ 分

- 16. 午前中に、外あそびをしていますか？
- 17. 15時～17時くらいの時間帯に、外でしっかり遊んでいますか？
- 18. 走ったり、跳んだり、ボールを投げたりを、バランスよくしていますか？
- 19. 鉄棒やうんていにぶら下がったり、台の上で、バランスをとったりしていますか？
- 20. 園庭や公園の固定遊具で、楽しく遊んでいますか？

⑤发展的均衡性

运动篇

⑤ 发展的均衡（身体的、社会的、智力的、精神的、情绪的）

「是否有保护自己身体的体力、是否能和人友好相处、是否能在游戏玩法上下功夫、是否有能够努力到最后的决心、是否能够忍耐等，需要我们一一确认孩子在游戏中被培养起来的诸多能力。」

发展的均衡性
（身体的・社会的・智力的・精神的・情绪的）

- 21. 当孩子摔倒的时候，能收起下颌用手撑着地来保护身体吗？（身体的・自我保护的能力）
- 22. 能和朋友一起开开心心地玩耍吗？（社会的）
- 23. 能够在游戏的玩法上下功夫，开心地玩耍吗？（智力的）
- 24. 玩耍完之后整理东西能坚持到最后吗？（精神的）
- 25. 即使是和人发生碰撞，能够控制自己的情绪吗？（情绪的）

回答"是"计1分，5分为满分。 共 ☐ 分

- 21. お子さんは、転んだときに、あごを引き、手をついて、身をかばうことができますか？
- 22. 友だちといっしょに関わって、なかよく遊ぶことができていますか？
- 23. あそび方を工夫して、楽しく遊んでいますか？
- 24. 遊んだ後の片づけは、最後までできますか？
- 25. 人とぶつかっても、情緒のコントロールができますか？

⑥父母的作用与支持

运动篇

⑥ 父母的作用与支持

「幼儿期的生活会依据父母关心与关注的不同而有很大变化。越多给孩子肯定的态度，亲子在一起的时间也会多起来，这对于亲子各自的身心健康都有良好的效果。」

父母的作用与支持

- 26. 有创造进行亲子活动的机会吗？
- 27. 注重在户外玩耍（家周围或公园等）的机会吗？
- 28. 比起坐车，有坚持陪孩子一起徒步出行吗？
- 29. 有和孩子随着音乐一起跳舞或做体操、做手指操吗？
- 30. 有努力让孩子1天做30分种以上的运动吗？

回答"是"计1分，5分为满分。 共 [　] 分

- 26. 親子で運動して、汗をかく機会を作っていますか？
- 27. 外（家のまわりや公園など）で遊ぶ機会を大切にしていますか？
- 28. 車で移動するよりは、お子さんと歩いて移動することを心がけていますか？
- 29. 音楽に合わせての踊りや体操、手あそびにつきあっていますか？
- 30. 1日に30分以上は、運動させるようにしていますか？

3．雷达图的填写方式

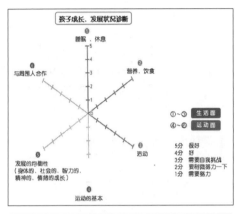

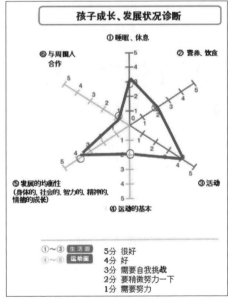

4 什么是体力

体力 (physical fitness)

- ①战胜威胁健康的外部刺激以保持健康的能力。
  （防卫体力）
  - 对疾病的抵抗力
  - 对炎热与寒冷的适应力
  - 对病原菌的免疫力　等等。
- ②运动时所需要的、能让身体积极活动的能力。
  （行动体力）

- 体力＝防卫体力+行动体力

行动体力的分类

◆ 使动作产生
1. 肌肉力量 (Strength: kg)
2. 爆发力 (Power)

◆ 保证动作正确进行 （调整力）
1. 协调性 (Coordination)
2. 平衡性 (Balance)
3. 敏捷性 (Agility)
4. 灵巧性 (Skillfulness)

● 动作的持久力
1. 肌肉的耐力 (Muscular endurance)
2. 心肺(呼吸、循环)功能的耐力、全身的耐力 (Cardiovascular/respiratory endurance)

● 动作顺利婉转地进行
1. 柔韧性 (Flexibility)
2. 节奏感 (Rhythm)

「吃、动、充足睡眠!」运动的目的－孩子成长发育的诊断与评价－　　205

Q：想要提升体力，怎么办才好呢？

为了提升体力
体力を向上させるためには

- 除了饮食（营养）和睡眠（休息）
- 增强体力维持健康、对能够精力充沛地进行活动起重要作用的是运动！
- 在运动或体育活动中，适度地使用身体很重要。
- Recreation效果（转换心情、恢复疲劳、对家庭生活的贡献）
　　→ training 效果（疲劳感）：体力提升
　　　　→ over training（过劳）
　　　　　　→ 生病
- 通过提高运动技能，能够让幼儿更加容易地体会到运动的快乐，同时也增加自我实现的机会。

- 食事（栄養）と睡眠（休養）のほか、
- 体力を増強させて健康を維持し、元気に活動するのに役立つのは、運動！
- 運動やスポーツで、身体を適度に使うことが大切
- レク効果（気分転換・疲労回復・家庭生活への寄与）
　→トレーニング効果（疲労感）：体力向上
　　→オーバートレーニング（過労）
　　　→病気
- 運動スキルを向上させることによって、スポーツをより楽しく行うことを可能にし、自己実現の機会も増えていく。

从小开始,
让孩子毫无偏颇地体验
4种运动技能!

不只是体力,也要锻炼
运动技能!

基本运动技能

- 移动类运动技能
- 操作类运动技能
- 平衡类运动技能
- 非移动类运动技能

5．体力和运动能力的不同

Q：体力和运动能力有什么不同呢？

体力是充分发挥肌肉力量、耐力、柔韧性、灵敏性等时机体的内在机能。运动能力是像跑、跳、投这样的活动，在体力基础上，加上进行运动与体育活动所必需的基本技能在里面。

体力は、筋力や持久力、柔軟性、敏捷性など、それらを発揮する際のスキルをできるだけ排除した形でとらえた生体の機能を意味する。
運動能力は、走、跳、投といった、体力に、運動やスポーツに必要な基本的なスキルを加味した能力を意味する。

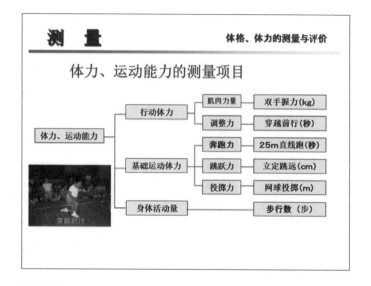

① 双手握力值

• 两脚叉开,让幼儿用两手使尽全身的力气握握力器。

• 施测2次,记下成绩最好的一次。

② 穿越前行

- 拉上一根与幼儿膝盖同高的橡皮筋,从上面跳过去之后,立刻从下面钻过返回原地,连续做5次,记下总共所需时间。

③ 25M直线跑

- 让幼儿跑30m长的路线,记录在25m处的通过时间。

④ 网球掷远

- 使用硬式网球，让幼儿尽量往远投。
- 实施2次，记录成绩好的一次。

⑤ 立定跳远

- 使用垫子，两脚同时蹬地向前方跳出，测得所跳距离。
- 施测2次，记录成绩好的一次。

演讲

公园内运动器材的重要性

前桥 明

早稻田大学
教授/医学博士

日本幼儿体育学会
会长

212 Part III

我们开发的运动器材

和福禄贝尔公司一起开发

公园内运动器材的重要性　213

协调性

和若越公司一起开发

基本运动技能

- 移动类运动技能
- 操作类运动技能
- 平衡类运动技能
- 非移动类运动技能

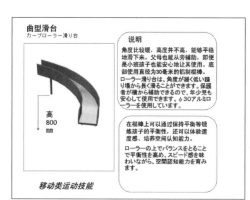

移动类运动技能

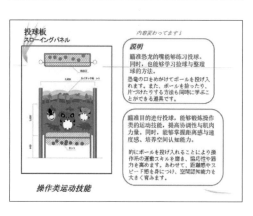

操作类运动技能

公园内运动器材的重要性 215

圆柱台阶
四段円柱ステップ

高 600 mm

説明

主要用于低年龄幼儿。采用圆柱形的设计,可以让孩子一边保持平衡一边攀登。

低年齢児用のステップです。円形のステップをバランスをとりながら、登ります。

通过不同高度的登上登下可以锻炼孩子的肌肉力量与平衡性,并培养孩子的节奏感。

ステップを登り降りすることで筋力や平衡性を育みます。登り降りしながら、リズム感も養うことができます。

平衡类运动技能

吊环云梯

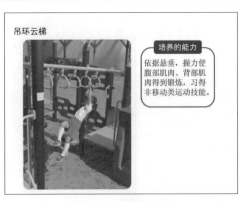

培养的能力

依据悬垂,握力使腹部肌肉、背部肌肉得到锻炼,习得非移动类运动技能。

大恐龙(细长型)

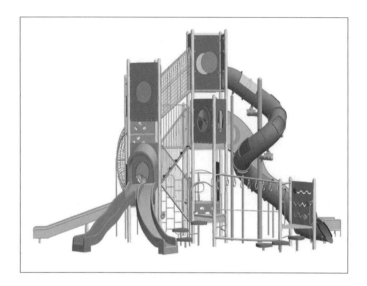

为了培养全面发展的孩子

通过多种多样的游戏或活动以及指导,培养社会人(人间形成)。

- 身体的 (physical)
- 社会的 (social)
- 智力的 (intellectual) mental
- 精神的 (spiritual)
- 情绪的 (emotional)

公园内运动器材的重要性　219

均衡发展
(身体的・社会的・智力的・精神的・情绪的)

1. 能手脚并用在大型的运动器具上，登上登下、钻爬或悬垂吗？
2. 能和小伙伴一起和谐地玩耍吗？
3. 能在玩法儿上下功夫吗？
4. 能够坚持到最后到达目的地吗？
5. 能在最后登上大型器具时感受到爽快感和释放感，以充分舒解情绪么？

- 1. 手足をフルに使って、遊具を登ったり、降りたり、くぐったり、ぶら下がったりできますか？
- 2. 友だちといっしょに関わって、なかよく遊ぶことができていますか？
- 3. 登り方や下り方、あそび方を工夫して、楽しく遊んでいますか？
- 4. 目的地点まで、最後まで行くことができますか？
- 5. 最後まで登り切ったときの爽快感や解放感を味わい、情緒の解放を図っていますか？

1　身体面

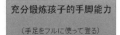

蜗型爬网
ワイドエスカルゴネット

充分锻炼孩子的手脚能力
（手足をフルに使って登る）

2 社会面

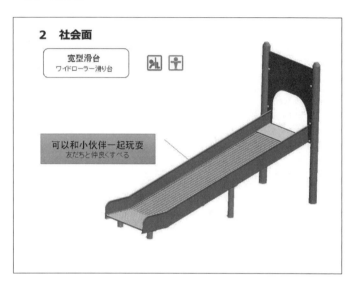

宽型滑台
ワイドローラー滑り台

可以和小伙伴一起玩耍
友だちと仲良くすべる

3 智力面

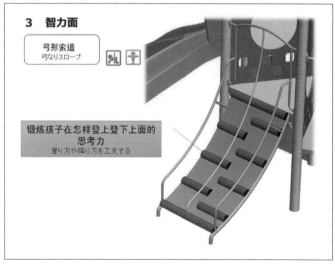

弓形索道
弓なりスロープ

锻炼孩子在怎样登上登下上面的思考力
登り方や降り方を工夫する

公园内运动器材的重要性　221

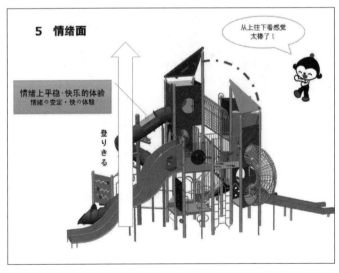

设计幼儿园户外场地 ～提高幼儿运动能力的庭院设计～

户外场地设计的7个要点　　1
(園庭デザインの7つのポイント 1)

1.综合运动器材和大型运动器材，设置在离教室较远的位置。
1.総合遊具や大型遊具は、園舎から遠い位置に配置する。

到了活动时间，孩子们跑出教室奔向综合运动器材和大型运动器材。所以把运动器材尽量设置在离教室稍微远的地方，能够确保孩子有更多的运动量。

あそびの時間になると、子どもたちは園庭に駆け出し、総合遊具や大型遊具を目指します。大好きな総合遊具や大型遊具を、園舎から園庭のできるだけ離れた場所に配置することによって、子どもたちは、より多くの運動量を確保することができます。

户外场地设计的7个要点　　2
(園庭デザインの7つのポイント 2)

2. 户外场地中心点周围要留出足够的自由玩耍空间。
2.園庭の中心にトラック（スペース）を確保する

虽然是要考虑户外场地的规模，但是在户外场地里留出能够设置跑道的空间很重要。在此空间内孩子们不仅能够自由地跑动、也能够玩球或做游戏、提高孩子的灵敏性与协调性。

園庭の規模にもよりますが、トラックを設営できるくらいのフリースペースが大切です。子どもたちが、自由に駆け回ることができるだけでなく、球技やゲーム等を行って、器用さや協応性をアップさせ、協調性を育みます。フリースペースでのあそびは、運動量を増やし、想像力を伸ばすという点を見逃せません。

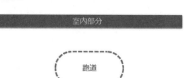

户外场地设计的7个要点　　3
（園庭デザインの7つのポイント３）

3. 考虑能够进行循环游戏活动的移动轨迹。
3.サーキットあそびができる動線を考慮する。

循环游戏是把好几种运动器械组合在一起，综合提高孩子体力与运动能力的综合性巡回游戏。我们要考虑循环游戏的移动轨迹来进行设计。从离教室近处开始依次向远处设置对身体负荷较高的器械，让孩子即便是没有老师的指导也能够自然地和小伙伴们一起玩耍。也要考虑到保育室的位置依据各年龄段来设置不同的路线模型，使得循环游戏得到更为有效的开展。

複数の遊具を組み合わせ、体力や運動能力を総合的にアップさせる巡回式のサーキットあそびのできる動線を設計したいものです。園舎側から、からだへの負荷の高い遊具を、徐々に設置していくことで、特に指導しなくても、しぜんと子どもたちはサーキットあそび を楽しみます。保育室の位置も考えながら、年齢別にモデルコースを設定すると、より効果的なサーキットあそびが展開されます。

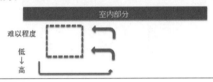

循环游戏活动
サーキットあそび

起点兼终点　スタート兼ゴール

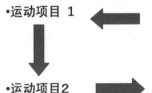

- 运动项目 1　　　　　运动项目 4

- 运动项目 2　　　　　运动项目 3

户外场地设计的7个要点　　4
（園庭デザインの7つのポイント4）

4. 能够提高体力和运动技能的小型运动器械需放置在园舍付近。
4.体力や運動スキルをつけていく遊具は、園舎の近くに配置する。

把对能够有效地提高孩子体力与习得运动技能的运动器材设置在离教室较近的地方。如果考虑孩子们游戏或运动时的行动轨迹并让孩子能够就近使用到，那么它的利用频率就会变高。这样，孩子的体力或运动能力等自然而然就会得到提高。

体力の向上と運動スキルの習得に有効な遊具を、園舎近くに置き、いつでも使ってもらえるように、あそびの動線に組み込んでいくと、利用頻度があがっていきます。そうすると、子どもの体力や運動能力は、自然とアップしていくのです。

户外场地设计的7个要点　　5
（園庭デザインの7つのポイント5）

5. 低年龄幼儿与高年龄幼儿分区域活动
5.低年齢児と幼児のエリア分けをする。

能够让孩子尽情地玩耍、充分地体验4种运动技能很重要。另一方面，因为3岁以下的孩子和3岁以上的孩子之间能力上有很大的差异，所以让他们在同一个区域玩耍的话，有时候会发生一些碰撞事故。那么，如果户外场地空间充裕的话，分区让孩子进行活动既安全又有效。审视教室、运动器械的设置以及运动轨迹的设置，能够减少事故确保安全。

子どもたちを思いっきり遊ばせ、4つの基本運動スキルを経験させていく必要がある反面、3歳未満児と3歳以上児との間には、大きな能力差があり、同じエリアで遊んでいると、接触による事故が起こることもあります。園庭に余裕があれば、エリア分けも安全で、かつ有効な方法です。教室・遊具の配置、動線の設計を見直すことで、事故を減らし、安全を確保することができるのです。

庭院设计的7个要点　6
（園庭デザインの7つのポイント6）

6. 建造一个没有死角的庭院。
6.管理者の死角がない園庭にする

　一个充满绿色和运动器材丰富的庭院，对于孩子来说是一件非常开心的事。但是如果设施设置过过满会成为危险隐患。所以有必要以教室一侧为视点无死角地设置运动器材或绿地等是很必要的。不仅能够防止孩子间的接触和运动器材的使用所带来的事故，对防范外来的危险也有效果。

遊具や緑がいっぱいの園庭は、園児にとって楽しいもの。しかし、詰め込みすぎは、危険を招くため、園舎側から見て死角のないように、遊具や緑地を設置する必要があります。子ども同士の接触や遊具での事故を防ぐだけでなく、防犯面からの効果も高めておきたいものです。

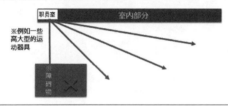

※例如一些高大型的运动器具

户外场地设计的7个要点　7
（園庭デザインの7つのポイント7）

7. 依据孩子的年龄考虑教室的设置
7.園舎の年齢別クラス配置を考慮する。

　我们要考虑到即便是孩子一下子跑出教室也能够安全地、顺利地进行活动这一点，来设计运动器械等的摆放。依据各个年龄段孩子的喜好、把受欢迎的中小型运动器械，孩子想玩的运动器械放在各个班级的近处。在此基础上考虑孩子的移动轨迹，对于循环游戏活动也能起作用。对于特别受欢迎的大型运动器材，可以设置在稍远的地方以自然而然地保证身体的活动量。

一斉に飛び出す園児たちが、安全で、スムーズに、あそびに入れるように、遊具の位置を検討します。年齢ごとに人気のある小型や中型の遊具、遊んでほしい遊具を、クラスの近くに設置します。その上で動線を考え、サーキットあそびにつなげていくのです。とくに人気のある大型遊具は、少し離れたところに設置して、身体活動量を自然に確保する方法が有効です。

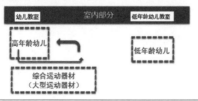

户外场地的设计 ～从户外场地的规模来看～

小型户外场地

因为小型的户外场地管理的范围比较小,所以保证安全的设置较为容易。但是,若是运动器械的配置错误的话,孩子们的运动轨迹就会重复,相互碰撞造成危险,应引起注意。

通常情况下,即便是难以确保运动量的小型户外场地,如果能够确保上述的设计的7个要点的话,也能够保证孩子充足的运动量,成为利用高效的户外场地。

小さい園庭は、管理する範囲が狭いので、安全な園庭デザインがしやすいです。しかし、遊具の配置をあやまると、子どもたちの動線が重なり、衝突を生じる危険となるので、注意が必要です。

通常は、運動量の確保が難しい小園庭でも、前述の7つのポイントを押さえれば、十分な運動量を確保でき、効率のよい園庭に早変わりします。

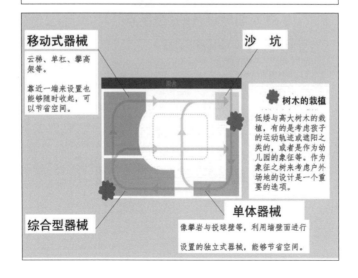

移动式器械
云梯、单杠、攀高架等。
靠近一端来设置也能够随时收起,可以节省空间。

沙坑

树木的栽植
低矮与高大树木的栽植,有的是考虑孩子的运动轨迹或遮阳之类的,或者是作为幼儿园的象征等。作为象征之树来考虑户外场地的设计是一个重要的选项。

综合型器械

单体器械
像攀岩与投球壁等,利用墙壁面进行设置的独立式器械,能够节省空间。

中型户外场地

符合各个园的理念及所在地区气候，会使运动器械的设置更加容易、也能够设计出整体上和谐的户外场地。如果能够遵循孩子的运动轨迹来配置独立式与综合式的运动器械的话，也能在提高孩子体力和运动能力上达到同大型户外器械相当的效果。

園の方針や地域の風土に合わせて、遊具を設営しやすく、まとまりのある園庭デザインが可能です。動線を意識して、単体遊具と総合遊具を効果的に配置すれば、大園庭なみの体力と運動能力アップも狙えます。

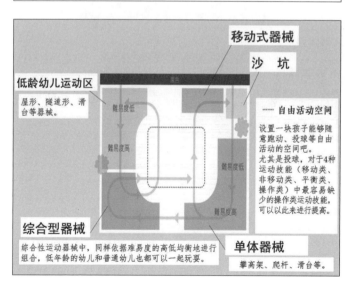

移动式器械

沙　坑

低龄幼儿运动区
屋形、隧道形、滑台等器械。

自由活动空间
设置一块孩子能够随意跑动、投球等自由活动的空间吧。
尤其是投球，对于4种运动技能（移动类、非移动类、平衡类、操作类）中最容易缺少的操作类运动技能，可以以此来进行提高。

综合型器械
综合性运动器械中，同样依据难易度的高低均衡地进行组合，低年龄的幼儿和普通幼儿也都可以一起玩耍。

单体器械
攀高架、爬杆、滑台等。

大型户外场地

作为标志性的并且是对于提高孩子的体力有很大作用的大型运动器械的设置，及符合孩子年龄与发展特点的安全活动区域的划分，考虑孩子的运动轨迹确保运动量等都可以成为户外场地设计的参考。因为需要管理的范围比较大，所以需要设置有高度的、有魅力的器械。

シンボリックで、かつ、体力づくりに寄与する大型遊具の設置や、年齢や発達に合わせた安全なエリア分け、動線を考慮し、運動量を確保できる園庭づくりが可能になります。管理する範囲が広いため、高度で、魅力的なレイアウトが求められます。

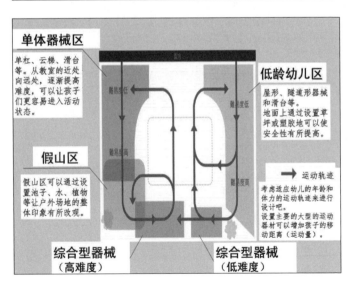

单体器械区
单杠、云梯、滑台等。从教室的近处向远处，逐渐提高难度，可以让孩子们更容易进入活动状态。

低龄幼儿区
屋形、隧道形器械和滑台等。地面上通过设置草坪或塑胶地可以使安全性有所提高。

假山区
假山区可以通过设置池子、水、植物等让户外场地的整体印象有所改观。

➡ 运动轨迹

考虑适应幼儿的年龄和体力的运动轨迹来进行设计吧。
设置主要的大型的运动器材可以增加孩子的移动距离（运动量）。

综合型器械（高难度）

综合型器械（低难度）

韩国的公园运动器材的介绍

台湾的公园运动器材

公园内运动器材的重要性

设置前需要考虑的事项或条件
設置に先立つ配慮・条件

- 为了能够让孩子们安全且顺畅地使用运动器械进行活动,要充分考虑孩子们的移动轨迹来进行完美的运动器械的设置。
- 避免迎头碰撞。
- 运动流不能极度地拥挤。
- 确保必要的活动空间(确保安全区域)极为重要。
- 这个空间内除了器械本身之外,不能有照明灯、井盖、路牙等设施、石头或玻璃等异物。

- 安全、かつ、スムーズに、遊具を使った楽しいあそびが展開できるよう、子どもたちの動きの流れ・動線や遊具の配置を周到に行う。
- 子どもたちが出合い頭にぶつからない。
- 運動の流れが極度につまらない。
- 活動に必要とされる空間を確保すること(安全区域の確保)が、極めて重要。
- この空間内には、遊具本体を除き、照明灯やマンホール、縁石などの施設や、石やガラス等の異物があってはならない。

公园内运动器材的重要性

设置保证安全的垫子

考虑安全性的固定运动器材的设计及其安全性
安全に配慮した固定遊具の設計と安全性

考虑安全性的运动器材的设计及其产品本身的安全性
安全に配慮した遊具の設計と製品そのものの安全性

考虑安全性的设计
- 充分考虑和利用花草树木等环境，确保安全区域是根本。
- 安全垫的设置或者是为了引起孩子的注意，在高低处、区域性地进行涂色区分等也是安全设计与配置中被要求的。

安全に配慮した設計
- 花や樹木などの環境を生かしつつ、安全エリアを確保することが基本となります。
- 安全マットの設置や段差・区域の注意喚起の塗り分け等、安全に配慮した設計・配置が求められます。

公园内运动器材的重要性 237

设计、设置上的注意事项
設計・設置上の留意点

① 防止卡住头、躯干、颈、手指
- 去除造成卡住头、躯干、颈、夹到手指等安全隐患的缝隙处，防止事故的发生。
- 孩子不能认识到自己身体的大小，所以他们想要通过某个狭小处时容易发生卡住头或身体的事故。为了避免这一事故的发生，把开口处设计成身体钻不进去，或者是躯干能钻进去头部也能钻进去的构造。

② 防止夹手指
　不设置能够伸进手指这样的小洞。

①頭部・胴体・首・指の挟みこみ
- 頭部・胴体・首・指を挟みこんでしまう隙間を除去して、事故を防止してもらいたいものです。
- 子どもが自分の体格を意識せずに通り抜けようとした場合、頭部や胴体の挟み込みが発生しないように、開口部は胴体が入らない構造にするか、胴体が入る場合は頭部が通り抜ける構造にしましょう。

②指の挟み込み
- 指が抜けなくなる恐れのある穴は設けない。

③ 防止夹到脚
- 缓冲区或通道等这样以走跑为目的设置的平坦地面之间的缝隙不要超过6mm。但是，像吊桥等以游戏为目的等器械的设计，缝隙要避免能够引起头部或躯干被卡住事故。
- 孩子们容易触碰到的地方不要设置突起部分或缝隙，以免面事故发生。

④ 防止被缠住、被刮扯住
- 孩子容易触碰到的部分，必须考虑到不要缠住或扯住书包带儿、衣服的一部分等。特别是像滑走类的运动器械的滑出部分，在预想落下的地方不设容易被缠住的突起部或缝隙。为了防止掉落的危险可以设置一些栅栏等。

③足の挟み込み
- 踏み場や通路といった歩行や走行を目的とした平坦な床面の隙間は、6 mmを超えないようにしましょう。ただし、つり橋やネット遊具等のあそびを目的とした部分の隙間は、頭部や胴体の挟み込みが起こらないようにしてもらいます。
- 要は、子どもが容易に触れる部分には、突出部や隙間を除去し、事故を防止したいものです。

④絡まり、引っ掛かり
- 子どもが容易に触れる可能性のある部分には、着衣の一部やカバンのひもが絡まったりしないように配慮しなければなりません。とくに、滑走系の遊具のすべり出し部分のように、落下が予想される箇所では、絡まったり、引っかかったりする突出部や隙間がないようにしてください。高さに応じて、ガードレールや落下防止柵を設置し、不意な落下を防止します。

维修及其使用方法
メンテナンスと使い方

1. 为了安全，日常的维修是很重要的。
   日常维修的实施、定期检查、依赖专业人员进行维修或改善。
2. 即便是安全的运动器械如果使用方法错误的话，同样会造成事故。
   ①了解运动器械的安全使用方法。
   ②依据此来指导孩子们。

1. 遊具を安全に利用するためには、日頃からのメンテナンスが重要。
   日常のメンテナンスの実施、定期点検、専門家に依頼しての修理や改善。
2. 安全な遊具の使い方を誤ると、ケガや事故が起こる。
   ①遊具の安全な使い方を知ること、
   ②それらの基本を、使う子どもたちにも指導しておくことが求められる。

对于小孩子的教导
子どもへの指導

· 用正确的方法使用运动器械，和其他小朋友和平共处一起玩。
· 早发现问题早解决可以有效防止事故的发生，需要大人来配合。
· 从幼儿期开始就教孩子们，如果螺丝脱落或有奇怪的声音发出，要马上告知大人。
· 使用运动器械，若在使用上感觉到有什么不对的地方马上联系老师。

· 遊具は、正しい使い方をして、仲良く遊ぶ。
· 早期発見・早期対応が事故防止に繋がるので、大人の協力が必要。
· ねじが緩んでいたり、異音が生じたりするときは、子どもも、すみやかに近くにいる大人に伝えるよう、幼少児期から指導しておくことが重要。
· 遊具を利用していて、不具合や異変を感じたら、先生（管理者）に連絡をすること。

報告結束。
感謝聆聽。

谢 谢
감사합니다
Terima kasih banyak
Thank you again for the present!
あいがとうございました
早稲田大学 前橋 明でした！

Profile of Prof. Akira MAEHASHI

Akira MAEHASHI
Doctor of Medicine
Waseda University, Professor
Japan Society of Leisure and Recreation Studies, Chief Director
Japan Society of Physical Education of Young Children, Chairperson
2005 & 2018 Asian Society of Physical Education of Young Children, Chairperson
International Society of Physical Education of Young Children, Chairperson

Resume
1978 University of Missouri-Columbia, Graduate School, Master Degree (Education)
1996 Okayama University, Medical School, Doctorate Degree (Medicine)
Kurashiki City College (1987 Lecturer, 1992 Assistant Professor, 2000 Professor)
University of Missouri-Columbia, Visiting Researcher
University of Vermont, Visiting Professor

Taiwan National Sports University, Visiting Professor
Current: 2003 Waseda University, Professor

Research Works

Major research surrounding the relationship between fatigue and body temperature in children, lifestyle rhythm of toddlers, about parental stress as a result of childcare and child support.

To contribute the findings and results of the research to the well-being, care and education for children and the application of such findings to children in Asia for a better and healthier future for children of the region.

At the same time, to tackle various health and well-being problems faced by children by carrying out nationwide surveys and research on young children's health and lifestyle surveys.

Awards

1992 Honorary Citizen Award

    Kansas City Missouri U.S.A.

1998 Research Award

    Japan Society of Research on Early Childhood Care and Education

2002 Special Contribution Award

    Japanese Society of Health Education of Children

2008 Best Thesis Award

    Japanese Society of Health Education of Children

2008 Well-being Award

    Japan Society for Well-being of Nursery-schoolers

2016 Kids Design Award (10th)

    Kids Design Council, etc

前桥 明教授的简介

医学博士
早稻田大学教授
日本幼儿体育学会 会长
2005·2018 亚洲幼儿体育学会 会长
国际幼儿体育学会 会长

学位
1978年毕业于美国密西里大学 硕士学位（教育学）
1996年毕业于日本岗山大学 博士学位（医学）

曾任
仓敷市短期大学教授
美国密西里大学客座研究员
美国弗蒙特大学客座教授
台湾国立体育大学客座教授

研究领域
　　儿童疲劳与体温的关系、婴幼儿的生活习惯、父母的育儿疲劳与援助，近年来把以上研究内容应用于儿童福祉领域，促进幼少儿的健康发展、并在日本全国和亚洲部分地区做关于幼少儿健康和生活实际状况的调查。

获得荣誉
1992年　美国堪萨斯市荣誉市民奖
1998年　日本保育学会研究奖励奖
2002年　日本幼少儿健康教育学会功劳奖
2008年　日本幼少儿健康教育学会优秀论文奖
2016年　第10回儿童运动器材设计大奖

■著　者

　日本幼儿体育学会　前桥　明　（JAPAN）
　（早稲田大学　教授　医学博士）

■译　者

　北京绿树体育　孙研・潘磊・马天雪・郑微（CHINA）

■英文校阅

　Thomas Comet Halley (U.S.A.)

■中文校阅

　姜　碧莹（早稲田大学　大学院）

■協　力　ジャクエツ環境事業
　　　　　ジャクパ

幼儿体育与健康 ― 让孩子运动、心动、感动

2018年11月20日　初版第1刷発行

■著　　者――日本幼児体育学会
　　　　　　　前橋　明
■訳　　者――北京緑樹体育
■イラスト――大森和枝
■発 行 者――佐藤　守
■発 行 所――株式会社 大学教育出版
　　　　　　　〒700-0953　岡山市南区西市855-4
　　　　　　　電話（086）244-1268　FAX（086）246-0294
■印刷製本――モリモト印刷㈱

©Akira Maehashi 2018, Printed in Japan
検印省略　　落丁・乱丁本はお取り替えいたします。
本書のコピー・スキャン・デジタル化等の無断複製は著作権法上での例外を除き禁じられています。本書を代行業者等の第三者に依頼してスキャンやデジタル化することは、たとえ個人や家庭内での利用でも著作権法違反です。
ISBN978-4-86429-534-5